T0127185

LETTERS TO YEYITO

LESSONS FROM A LIFE IN MUSIC

LETTERS TO YEYITO

LESSONS FROM A LIFE IN MUSIC

Paquito D'Rivera

Translated from the Spanish
by Rosario Moreno

RESTLESS BOOKS
Brooklyn, New York

Copyright © 2015 Paquito D'Rivera
Translation copyright © 2014 Rosario Moreno
Digital edition published by Restless Books, 2015
This edition published by Restless Books, 2015

All rights reserved.

No part of this book may be reproduced or transmitted
without the prior written permission of the publisher.

Cover and book design by Jonathan Yamakami

ISBN: 978-1-63206-0-198

Ellison, Stavans, and Hochstein LP
232 3rd Street, Suite A111
Brooklyn, NY 11215

www.restlessbooks.com
publisher@restlessbooks.com

Contents

LETTERS TO YEYITO

LESSONS FROM A LIFE IN MUSIC

Dear Yeyito

No one sends letters anymore, not by mail, messenger, or any other way. Like smoke signals, perfumed envelopes are things of the past. Teletype noises have been muted, and I don't think telegrams even exist anymore! Now technology avails us with email, voicemail, and those text messages! Kids have turned spelling into something impractical, unnecessary, and obsolete with their symbols, codes, and abbreviations. Yes, everything is easier now, and the romance of the old-fashioned epistle, impeccable handwriting, and the unique, personal signature has been lost. However, it was precisely such a letter, written by an unknown person and as of yet unanswered, that motivated me to write this book.

In April 1967, after years of considering jazz to be "imperialistic music" (for reasons that were never clear), the Cuban National Council of Culture decided to authorize the formation of the Orquesta Cubana de Música Moderna—the Cuban Orchestra of Modern Music, of which I was a founding member. The big band format was typically American, and its vast repertoire included a range of well-known jazz pieces, international pop, Cuban music, and what is today called "Top 40."

Instruments were imported from Europe, Canada, and Japan, the most outstanding musicians of the genre were gathered, and Armando Romeu, a true icon in jazz circles on the island, was chosen as musical director. Romeu, who came from an illustrious musical family, had directed the Tropicana Night Club's orchestra for twenty-five years. Internationally renowned artists such as Edith Piaf, Johnny Mathis, Celia Cruz, Benny Moré, Josephine Baker, Carmen Miranda, Maurice Chevalier, Sarah Vaughan, and Nat King Cole had performed under his direction.

To give it the "proper" political tone, the Cuban government planned the Orquesta Cubana de Música Moderna's grand debut in Guane, a tiny remote town located on the westernmost extreme of the island. Guane's most illustrious and memorable "son" was perhaps the great and famous "*charanguero*" flutist, José Fajardo.

After the debut, several tours of the country took place, including turbulent concerts at Havana's Amadeo Roldán and Karl Marx Theaters. People would kill to come in and listen to Count Basie's blues and Joseíto Fernández "La Guantanamera" along with songs by The Beatles, Ray Charles, and other foreign artists. Later, the government ordered the formation of similar orchestras in the interior provinces.

Although the fervor was about as short-lived as the official support, which lasted almost two years, the public was still hungry for the happy, snazzy music and followed the splendid orchestra with enthusiasm. They knew the names of songs and musicians by heart. "Mint Julep," recorded by Ray Charles in 1961 was the biggest hit, and the not-so-young of that era may still remember it nostalgically.

Directed by Armando Romeu and Rafael Somavilla (an extraordinary pianist and arranger from Matanzas), the band members became role models, and many aspiring musicians followed Chucho's agile fingers, Carlos Emilio's electrifying guitar, Arturo Sandoval's high notes, Juan Pablo Torres's unadulterated "trombonism," the restless strings of Cachaito's bass, and Enrique Plá's overwhelming skills on trap drums.

It was during those days of youth and success that I received a letter written with the simplicity and ingenuity typical of country folk. This letter had the passion of someone who wanted above all else to achieve something in life. The writer was either a young music student or an aspiring one, from a small town lost in the center of our island. He described his emotions, while at our concert in Santa Clara's Teatro de la Caridad, intensely narrating how, after traveling all day and many kilometers from his hometown, he miraculously entered the theater across from Vidal Park in Santa Clara, which was packed wall-to-wall.

I tried to see you after the concert, but they didn't let me in. I was pushed around and shoved against the dark, dingy walls of a narrow hallway. They tore my shirt and attacked me, and I was almost strangled with my own tie. It was a huge screaming crowd! I had even brought you a pair of mameys that your uncle Ernesto told me you liked, but in all the mayhem they flew out of my hands and wound up smashed by the feet of the mob.

It was true that I loved mameys, the red and brown fruit, rough on the outside and sweet and tender inside, also known as *zapote* in other regions of the Americas. My uncle Ernesto, a funny and gregarious individual who traveled regularly from Havana to Santiago in his ten-wheeler, had evidently talked about our blood relation.

The truth is, I was about eighteen at the time and couldn't have known how to answer his questions: "What do you like best about the metal Selmer mouthpiece you use? Do you study music theory? How do you play the high notes with confidence? How do you know where to play blues notes when improvising?"

I wouldn't have known how to answer because I always did those things spontaneously, without thinking. He also wanted to know if I ever got stage fright, but the most confusing question he asked was "Is it a worthwhile pursuit to become a professional musician?"

I finished reading his letter with tears in my eyes and a sensation of pride and joy in my soul, but also frustration. Apparently, in his enthusiasm, Yeyito had forgotten to write his return address. It would have been hard to find that tiny remote town on the map of our long, narrow island, shaped like a sleeping Cayman. He had just signed "Yeyito."

Needless to say, Yeyito, I never got to meet you or find out if you made a musical career for yourself—either in Cuba or elsewhere, as many of us have. When I remember fragments of your letter, I can't help but feel as one might feel walking upon the sand of a New York beach some afternoon, under a gray sky, freezing hands in pockets, and finding a letter written decades ago inside a bottle washed ashore. Except that now it is I who throws the bottle into the water, hoping that someday it'll reach your hands across the oceans.

I owe you an apology for taking more than four decades to answer your letter—although you do share part of the blame, since you forgot to write at least your last name and return address on the envelope you sent with that mysterious messenger who put it under my door in Marianao and disappeared without a trace. A small detail that would have made things a bit faster, don't you think? But, as they say, better late than never. I will now take advantage of globalization and the Internet, which makes it so much easier for people to communicate, hoping these words will reach you and answer your questions. I will start with whether it was worth it to pursue the musical career that has so generously filled my spirit and stomach for so many years.

Dizzy Gillespie

One of the artists who most influenced my career (and that of many others) was John Birks "Dizzy" Gillespie. To be honest, we didn't like the first bebop recording my father brought home when I was a child. It was one of those ten-inch LPs, of the Charlie Parker Quintet with Max Roach on the drums, Curley Russell on bass, Miles Davis on the trumpet, and Dizzy playing piano. Dizzy told me later that the pianist was supposed to be Bud Powell but he never showed up.

I can still remember my old man reasoning, "My God! What were they playing that clashed with everything we had listened to before? It didn't remotely sound like the Benny Goodman Orchestra, Ellington, Artie Shaw, the Dorsey brothers, or Al Gallodoro. But you can tell they are good musicians, right?"

In time, those creative improvisers wound up captivating all of us, becoming an important part of our lives and our professional formation. Although I never met Bird (as they called Parker), Curley, or Miles, I did have the opportunity to work with Max a couple of times and had a tight personal and professional relationship with Dizzy until he left us in 1993.

He was a fun and naturally generous guy, encouraging his colleagues' educational and professional advancement. Dizzy was an inspiration until the day he died. I wrote a bossa nova titled "A Night in Englewood" dedicated to him. Englewood was the New Jersey town where he lived his final years.

Dizzy Gillespie had such natural grace and an original sense of humor that he made us laugh until the very day of his funeral. The main chapel inside the ultra-modern Saint Peter's Church on Lexington Avenue in Manhattan was full, bursting with relatives, friends, fans, celebrities, and reporters, as well as those who were just curious and had crashed the service, drawn by the charismatic character who succumbed to pancreatic cancer on January 6, 1993. That also happened to be his wife Lorraine's birthday.

In the front row of the semicircular structure, devastated by pain and surrounded by her loved ones, was Lorraine, the woman who had been by the trumpet player's side for more than five decades. Her gaze lost in the emptiness around her, as she stood motionless before the coffin. Behind the widow, flanked by his wife Andrea and pianist Mike Longo, who was crying inconsolably, was Ed Cherry. The very tall guitarist had accompanied the southern musician during the last years of his brilliant career, and now this enormous piece of humanity was plopped down on a wooden bench, all dressed in black, tears streaming down his face.

"Hi, Paquito. I'm Lalo Schifrin," the composer of *Gillespiana* and the famous theme from the television series *Mission: Impossible* introduced himself. We hugged as we cried over the coffin of our beloved maestro, boss, and friend. And that is how I finally met the Argentinean composer with whom I had chatted on the phone so many times and developed a beautiful musical and personal association. The fact remains that in a world such as ours, with such propensity towards discord and rotten apples, John Birks "Dizzy" Gillespie was a unifying element even in death.

There was one piece of jewelry Dizzy always wore on his chest and never took off. He wore it with a tuxedo or a dashiki or even a bathing suit. (Our mutual friend, Swiss entrepreneur Jacques Muyal, acquired it in 2005 at an auction in New Jersey.) It seemed to be an irregularly shaped calcareous stone, three to four inches long, beautifully intertwined with a sort of gold net and attached to a hoop that hung from a thick chain of the same metal.

Someone right behind me shouted, "Look at that, they've hung the mammoth tooth that the African king gave him around his neck!"

I thought to myself, "He can't be talking about the moon rock Dizzy told me he got at NASA." Dizzy's cousin Boo Frasier walked away from Lorraine to join our group around the sarcophagus and appeared surprised.

"African king? Mammoth? Well, he told me it was a petrified finger from a volcano eruption in Pompeii, but Lorraine herself told me she thought it was a kidney stone from the sperm-whale his friend Charlie Whale brought from Greenland… Hmmm, you never know with Diz."

"This here? Ah yes, it is my beloved uncle… I mean rather, what's left of my Uncle Elmo," Gillespie said in earnest to the exotic television presenter who was interviewing him live on TV.

"Your Uncle Elmo? What on earth do you mean?" she asked.

"Well, yes, my Uncle Elmo was an incorrigible cannibal," Dizzy replied.

A puzzled look came over the lovely face of the light-skinned black woman, as Birks continued.

"Well, as you know, all of us blacks are cannibals, even though the majority of us have learned to control our impulses in order to fit into civilized society, right?"

The reporter's eyes widened and her jaw dropped almost down to her chest, as Dizzy continued straight-faced.

"Things stayed more or less under control until, one day, several of Uncle Elmo's neighbors began to disappear from his fashionable neighborhood, and although the police had no idea what was going on, our family knew full well the reason for the disappearances."

The host's pupils dilated even more.

"In those days, people were celebrating New Year's Eve, and since the crisis became unmanageable, all the members of our family came to a dramatic decision."

There was such silence in the studio you could hear the interviewer swallowing air. Dizzy took a deep breath as he twirled the jewel around his fingers. He gazed downward at the floor and, looking up suddenly right into the eyes of the girl, who now seemed to be in shock, he pronounced very somberly, "I remember that night, all the women in the family accompanied the main dish with a delicious menu that consisted of yellow rice, avocado, watercress salad, and red beans that our uncle had learned to savor after spending a few years in Puerto Rico. He worked on the island as general manager of the San Juan Morgue. Uncle Elmo was a devout Christian, so after Grandma recited the proverbial prayer, we ate him, roasted, for Christmas Eve dinner. Since Uncle was so little and chubby, he looked like a piglet with an apple in his mouth, the way you serve it traditionally on festive occasions."

The reporter, badly concealing a grimace, was at a loss for words. She shrugged her shoulders and gave a sigh that sounded like the snarling of a beast about to be sacrificed.

"After dinner, each of us kept a piece of Uncle Elmo as a personal memento. His brother Jonah, who was a great silversmith, stayed in his basement all night and part of the following morning designing a beautiful piece of jewelry like this, one for each member of the family. Oh Uncle Elmo, how we miss you!"

Gillespie concluded with his gaze glued to the tips of his fake ostrich skin boots and an expression of pain and nostalgia across his scrunched-up lips. For a few seconds, time seemed to stand still. There was absolute silence in the studio. A moment later, Dizzy looked up with those mischievous child eyes darting around to relish the stunned faces of his audience. The producer's shout, "Cut!" was the preamble to general laughter.

"And if you can believe that, you can believe anything!" said the trumpeter, laughing loudly.

In short, it was not a mammoth's molar or volcanic finger, anthropophagus uncle, or sperm whale kidney stone. The beautiful jewel Dizzy Gillespie wore around his neck was a marine stone that Andrea, the charming wife of guitarist Ed Cherry, mounted on a gold base she herself had made and gave as a gift to the trumpet player, who now seemed to smile from his casket, as if to laugh at us all.

I met Dizzy under circumstances so peculiar that they inspired me to write a short story, part reality, part fiction.

Sherlock Holmes in Havana

Elementary, my dear Watson.
—Arthur Conan Doyle

It was one of those sunny, windy Havana afternoons in April. In any other country just a bit further north, that might mean nothing more than temperatures somewhere between refreshing and warm. Depending on the subtle atmospheric variations of spring, we might even speak about some small, timid clouds that would cut a delicate white curtain of raindrops, graciously woven with the setting sun's fine gold fibers (romantic, isn't it!). However, the Caribbean is a whole other story. April may be as hellish as August, or stormy enough to provoke a desperate request of Noah for the blueprints of his lifesaving vessel.

Now, on this particular day, after it had rained something akin to what had fallen on the Ark, there was so much sun in Havana I thought it could crack a rock. I had been recording all morning with Elena Burke at EGREM studios, on San Miguel Street between Campanario and Lealtad. When it rained, the national label's ancient studio had leaks that competed with

Trevi Fountain's gargoyles in Rome, and the air conditioning was hardly working perfectly.

Even so, it was much more pleasant inside than outside, where the scalding heat made it possible to fry an egg on the hood of a car (in the event you could find an egg in hungry and ruined Havana). I knew this because between songs we would go out on the terrace to poison our lungs with nicotine and the horrible stench wafting from the nearby bathrooms, whose lack of water contrasted with the incredible humidity.

The recording session had been long and laborious. The damn tape machine would get stuck every now and then, the tape would unravel, and Tony López, the engineer, was at wit's end trying to make that piece of prehistoric electronics work. We were finally forced to stop. I left, ravenously hungry and in a foul mood. My stomach was screeching like the scratching old man Oscar Valdés had been doing on the güiro for one of the *danzónes* we were taping for Elena. I got up, put my saxophone in its case, and left like a dog looking for a bone.

I had to make an urgent phone call, but my paranoia kept me from using the phone at the studio. I went downstairs, and, just as I got to the door, I glanced tentatively toward the silent phone waiting for me on a gray metallic desk. I thought I'd better not, cautiously observing the man in the black beret behind the beat-up, grimy, ink-splattered desk reading a copy of the *Granma* newspaper. I didn't want anybody to have a clue about what I was up to and I was afraid that, even speaking in code, I might give away the secret, dangerous motive behind that call.

I forced a half smile and a wink to say goodbye to the man. When I got out to the narrow sidewalk, the rainstorm had stopped as quickly as it had begun, but instead of cooling things down, it had left a cloud of steam that felt like a Turkish bath. Now, with not a single cloud in that bluest of skies, the city was impregnated with the repugnant stench of burnt rubber. The humidity made my clothes stick to my skin; sweat ran down my face and fogged up my lenses.

I strolled toward the public phone on the wall outside the cafeteria at the corner of Campanario and checked to see that it was indeed, miraculously, working. I stress the miracle because finding a working phone in the capital in those days was like finding petrol (or water!) in your tub. The impoverished little eatery betrayed the anemic material emptiness that took up every inch of the once vibrant and noisy capital. Since there was a blackout, all of the neighborhood's radios had been silenced and the only sounds were from a hungry dog in the distance and the strident horn of one of the few buses left on Route 43—one of those that passed Neptuno Street once in a million years toward the far-off neighborhood of La Lisa, with people hanging off the doors and out the windows.

In spite of the day's blinding light, or perhaps for that very reason, the precarious little business was in shadows, and I was able to distinguish only the bright smile of the pretty, short young woman who attended to everyday nothingness from behind the well-worn counter. I thought I might choke from thirst, and, forgetting my important call for a moment, I practically begged the chubby girl for a glass of water.

She answered, her voice dripping with sarcasm, "Water? What planet are you living on, *mi corazón*? Better yet, wouldn't you rather have a ham and cheese *sangüichito* with a nice cold Coca-Cola?"

It had been years since anybody had offered me a sangüichito, and the words Coca-Cola sounded in my ears like the echo of a distant past, leaving me entranced for a few seconds by the effects of my hunger and thirst. I could still see the image of my rosy-cheeked, smiling teacher Rosita, and my jaw went slack with the memory of her extending the sangüichito and Coca-Cola they'd give us as a snack at the elementary school I attended in Marianao.

I must have been drooling when a guffaw from the chubby girl came from the shadows to wake me from my dreams and remind me that Centro Habana only got water a couple of times a week, brought in these huge, beat-up trucks everybody called *pipas*. Whenever anybody saw one of those trucks and yelled, "Waaaaaater," the neighborhood experienced something like the sailors who came over with Columbus must have experienced when Rodrigo de Triana, sitting atop the caravel's mast, screamed, "Land ho!"

The chubby girl, whose name was Yudislexis (ah, those Cuban names!) offered me a worn plastic glass with a yellowish liquid whose chemical composition would have been a mystery even to NASA scientists. This "brake fluid," as everybody called it, was nearly always available at places like that to wash down some even more mysterious fritters people called "Apollo 12 croquettes," like the American spaceship, because they insisted on defying gravity and sticking to the roof of your mouth. The brake fluid would assist the tongue in scraping the viscous substance and help break it down. That day, the astral croquettes were also available in the cafeteria, but since the oil ration to fry them hadn't arrived yet, and it had been more than a week since the gas truck had come by, it was impossible to cook and serve them. It was a Kafkaesque situation, or magic realism, as García Márquez would say, nodding his head as he lay by the pool at the impressive visitor's mansion the government had at his disposal in Miramar.

After thanking Yudislexis for the brake fluid, I excused myself and, after a good look around, picked up the receiver on the public phone to make my urgent call.

"The old man says you should get your ass over here and that your dresses are in the freezer."

The young man on the other end was Andresito, Andrés Castro's son, who, like his father, played trumpet. The "dresses" he referred to were meat his father got under the table from the neighborhood butcher. The butcher was part of an underground network for illegal meats (beef, chicken, pork), which was controlled by the very Committee in Defense of the Revolution that oversaw the tenement called El Trueno, or The Thunder, one of the rougher parts of the neighborhood.

"And don't take too long. The electricity's out until who knows when, and those dresses could spoil, you feel me?" Andresito added.

"Okay, I'm on my way," I said, hanging up the phone and laughing to myself as I tried to imagine the face of the police snitch listening in.

"Hey, music man... Want some Perla paste?" asked Yudislexis.

"Some what?" I asked loudly.

"Ssshhh, hey, lower your voice, baby. We're fucked if they hear us. Toothpaste, ten bills at the twins' place over at El Trueno. You know, those twins are something. They say that they stole a truck in daylight, right in front of the factory, and it was filled with bath soap, Perla toothpaste, Bebito cologne, and Snow White deodorant."

"Did you say Snow White deodorant?" I asked, knowing full well that the deodorant's brand name—if in fact it was deodorant—was a joke. "Hey, sweet thing," I said. "You tell the twins at El Trueno they should spill some of that Bebito cologne around here. It stinks so bad I wouldn't be surprised if Snow White's dwarves had died and their cadavers were rotting all over Havana."

The chubby gal laughed loudly. As she told me a story about her adolescent son, the result of a love affair with a Russian sailor, Yudislexis slowly but surely moved closer to me. A warm, salty breeze blew in from the sea and her long black hair softly caressed my face. Her exuberant and generous breasts brushed against my right arm, and I sincerely believed that Midas was a woman. Everything she touched with her magic tits turned to gold, making the misery all around disappear. In that moment, I could smell the deliciously fresh scent of the cologne combined with the delicate dew of her body; it had to be the same fragrance I'd smell in paradise.

"It's only ten pesos, *papichuli*," she whispered in my ear, as she dropped something in my pocket. "And for ten more, we can resurrect all those dead dwarves, whaddaya say?"

But then we heard (and saw) Yudislexis's boyfriend—a jealous, violent guy—about a block away. The brutish Mongo Mandarria, which was his *nom de guerre*, was pulling a rustic wooden cart on two old skates cut in half. On the cart was a fifty-gallon steel tank he filled with water whenever the trucks got to his block.

"Shit, it's so damn hot," I thought as I went down Campanario toward Ánimas, where the Castros lived. All the while I was trying to adjust the Bebito cologne bottle and the Perla toothpaste Yudislexis had shoved in my front jeans pocket. I thought to myself, "This girl's like an old stove; she gets you hot but doesn't cook." She got her way after all—never gave me what I wanted and ended up selling me something. It seemed like Mongo Mandarria always showed up at the moment of truth, dragging that damn cart, noisier than General Zhukov's tanks entering Berlin.

The heat and the humidity continued their assault, and the sax case on my back was weighing me down. For rather complicated reasons, I had to get rid of the original instrument case some time back. So a carpenter who specialized in coffins stole some materials from the funeral home where he worked and made me this new one: a strong wooden box lined with black vinyl, to which he'd attached a leather strap so I could throw it over my shoulder.

The carpenter's name was Nicolae, like his father, but the habaneros, who give everyone a nickname, simply called him Dracula. The poor guy had no choice but to respond to this macabre moniker. His grandfather Vlad Braunstein, a Jewish Romanian immigrant who had established a similar business back in Vienna, had not been able to return to his home in the '40s, first because the Nazis invaded Austria, then because the communists took over after World War II. The bloodthirsty General Basilescu's troops had shot his only son, his daughter-in-law, and two of their children in Bucharest, just as Vlad and his wife Mariana ran away with the youngest grandson to the Bulgarian side of the Danube. When they found out what had happened, the heartbroken Braunsteins made their way toward the Greek border and boarded a ship that crossed the Mediterranean and then the Atlantic to Cuba. The Braunsteins had a relative who had recently died in Havana, and left them a modest inheritance. But more importantly, the booming Jewish community in our city gave the new arrivals such a warm reception that the Romanian family was able to get ahead right away in our then-beautiful and welcoming capital.

With time and sacrifice, old man Braunstein managed to develop a successful business out of splendorous funerals— the Transylvania Funeral Home, whose slogan was "We don't want anyone to die, but we do want our business to prosper." The enterprise had its own carpentry shop, and little Nicolae, in spite of his autism, learned the craft of coffin making. When Castro's revolution arrived in 1959, the Transylvania Funeral Home, like other private businesses on the island, was taken over by the government.

Old man Braunstein, who could not fathom having come so far only to be ensnared again by the same evil, died from a wrenching heart attack after a violent argument with the government official who came to confiscate his business. Mariana lost her mind and was committed to Mazorra, the psychiatric hospital. And Dracula, who never understood a thing about politics, continued his work in the funeral home's carpentry shop, where the new government allowed him to keep a small room for himself. He lived and worked there completely alone.

The only problem was that Dracula, like so many with his condition, only learned to do one thing well, and obsessively. The case he made for me was a reproduction of a child's coffin. The maniac even carved a cross on the top! The mini-sarcophagus, as my friends referred to it, was incredibly heavy, and after a while it didn't feel like I was carrying an instrument but rather one of Snow White's dead dwarves.

I turned left at the corner of Ánimas, and halfway down the block, right at the Castros' door, I ran into Kemal Kairuz, the second-generation Lebanese pianist who played with Pablo Milanés at the Karachi before they hauled him off to the UMAP (*Unidades Militares de Ayuda a la Producción*) in Camagüey. I got goose bumps just thinking about the damn UMAPs. They were nothing less than forced labor camps, where they sent anybody with long hair, gays, and whoever else didn't fit into the revolutionary mold, anybody they considered "anti-social." That was back in the mid-'60s. Years later, Pablo came out of that hellhole and started singing praises to his jailers. Who can figure out people like that?

Kemal was rushing in the direction of the bodega on the next block; he was carrying a red bag with some Arabic lettering on the side. "Hey, Kemal, does that say, 'Thank you, Fidel' in Arabic or what?" I kidded him.

Arching his thick eyebrows with obvious glee he said, "Hey, man, don't mess with me. I'm on my way to Goyo's to get my stuff. They say the rice is here." Then, more confidentially, he added, "Damn, man, that rice is so bad I don't think even Mao Tse-Tung and his people could take it for two days straight. But I've got something to go with it today, like you, right?"

"How do you know?" I asked, half-serious, half-joking.

He looked up to the second floor, where Andrés's wife waved at us from the balcony, and answered, "Oh, you think you're the only one with the right to a relationship with protein?

You'd better go up. Our friend the trumpet player is waiting for you to start the show."

A squad car came down the narrow street very slowly; it seemed to me the officers were looking suspiciously at Kemal's unusual bag and the case Dracula had made for me. I also noted that there were more police on foot than usual. A little wary, I went up the stairs, my footsteps echoing, and felt like the cops were right on my heels.

"All this for red meat, which everybody says is bad because of the uric acid and what it does to the joints," I thought as I fled my imaginary pursuers. "But it's better to die from gout like a king, or go to prison, like the Count of Monte Cristo, than to die of hunger, like in Valeriano Weyler's concentration camps." I finally arrived, panting, on the second floor.

"Come on in, *Habichuela*," said Andrés with a little bow.

He'd been calling me Habichuela, or "green bean," since my days in the Estado Mayor General band, where I'd spent the three years of my military service. I was so thin in the olive-green uniform that I looked like a string bean. Andrés left me sitting in the living room and, because of the blackout, felt his way into the kitchen to pull the "dresses" from the freezer.

I'd already laid the ninety pesos on the table that the merchandise was going to cost me and now, Andrés unfolded a huge and bloody ball of newspaper before my avid and hungry eyes.

It was an eight- or ten-pound filet, more or less the equivalent to one year's worth of meat for a Cuban. We usually got about three-quarters of a pound of meat a month on the ration card—if the meat even got to the butcher shop. The long, cylindrical shape resembled a snake stripped of its skin. For a moment, there was the kind of contemplative silence usually reserved for great works of art or the passing of a great person.

"It looks like a donkey's penis," said Andresito.

"Young man, have some respect for your mother!" his father said.

"Look who's talking!" retorted the son.

"Yes, but she's not my mother—she's yours! In my day…"

"Oh, same difference," Andresito said to his father. "And anyway, I said penis, not dick, right?"

"Andresiiito!" exclaimed his mother Hildelisa.

I opened my mini-sarcophagus and stuffed into the mouth of my saxophone a halved onion and a few garlic cloves Andrés had given me, then the whole ball of meat, now wrapped in a cleaner piece of newspaper. The whole thing weighed so much that The Incredible Hulk could have used it to work out. I had to stuff the mouthpiece and the reed in the back pockets of my jeans, since I was carrying the cologne bottle and toothpaste the chubby girl had sold me in the front. These were joined by a piece of plantain and a small bag of beans Hildelisa gave me. Those pants, which were on the tight side, looked like they were going to burst.

Once I descended the stairs, I had to stop for a few seconds and let my eyes adjust, because the intense light from outside had temporarily blinded me. Andresito yelled down at me from the balcony, "Hey, Habichuela, if you boil that sax when you get home, you're gonna have quite the stew!"

I made like I had no idea what he was talking about and kept walking. The same squad car that had been cruising the neighborhood before I went up was coming by again, now even slower. In my crazy head, I imagined that the officers had been waiting the whole time to catch me with the irrefutable proof of my crime. I was terrified because I knew what would happen if I was caught with that "beeficide." But I didn't really have any other choice, so I kept walking, and without realizing it, I strolled right into a police raid on Ánimas at Perseverancia. I crossed Ánimas and turned right (I don't even know why exactly), toward the sea, where there were even more squad cars and a crowd in front of El Trueno.

The squad car I'd seen before had turned practically at the same time and came up slowly next to me. I continued for a few more meters on the sidewalk, and, not sure what to do, I stopped. Then out of nowhere came a paper bag full of shit that landed right on the hood of the squad car, exploding and spreading the nasty stuff all over the place. The driver quickly turned off the car, the doors popped open, and cops jumped out, guns in hand. My mouth went completely dry, and I felt my heart beating faster than it ever had in my life. But after looking me over for a second or two, the police officers— completely ignoring the fecal projectile that had just hit their vehicle—put their guns back in their holsters and went to join their brethren. While trying to hide the laughter provoked by the fantastic aim with which that unknown son of a bitch had launched the bag of shit, I got scared of what might happen if I backtracked, so I approached the tumult like someone with nothing to hide.

There were two very young mulattos in one of the squad cars who looked like they could be twins. One was shirtless, and the other had an Afro so big I thought they'd arrested Angela Davis. I found out the two combative mulattos were the illegitimate sons of Ramón Calzadilla, a distinguished operatic tenor who had a scandalous romance with a dark-skinned mulatta, an aging and frustrated *zarzuela* singer.

According to the story, Luisa Fernández, who was already a little old for motherhood, was hoping for twin girls, whom she planned on calling María and Calas. Things didn't turn out as she'd expected, and she decided to name her sons Plácido and Domingo, in honor of the great Spanish tenor. But given the bandits her sons turned out to be, they would have been better off with names like Don and Corleone or Lucky and Luciano.

Now, next to the squad car, the very thin, old mulatta, with gold teeth and dressed ever so skimpily, screamed hysterically for them to release her sons, who she claimed were innocent and one hundred-percent revolutionary. Her hair was on end, and the sparks glistening off her metallic mouth in the blazing Caribbean sun.

I was freaked and sweating up a storm, trying to figure a way out of there without drawing suspicion. Then I heard a nearby voice, musical, warm, raspy, and familiar: "Hey, *jabao lindo*, what are you doing in my neck of the woods?"

When I turned around, it was Juana Bacallao, who had for years lived in that miserable quarter, where such encounters with the police were commonplace. As was her custom, Juana was dressed to kill, as if she were about to step onstage at the Moulin Rouge in Paris. A platinum wig, long white gloves, a calf-length lamé dress, high heels, silk hose, a lace stole... She was smoking a *Populares* cigarette with her long, studded cigarette holder. Her face was resplendent in the sun, in spite of the various thick layers of makeup and a pair of dark-as-night glasses.

The effervescent image of Juana la Cubana swept away any fear, hunger, thirst, heat, or other suffering that might have affected me at that moment. There was a diminutive Chinese guy by her side who didn't say a word, a kind of miniature of incalculable age and delicate gestures who wore a pair of very tight black silk pants and a Japanese geisha blouse. It was Juana's personal valet-beautician, who was never far from her. I couldn't help but smile at the sui-generis pairing.

"And what are you laughing about? Do I have monkeys on my face or what?" asked Juana.

"Hmm, be careful, my brother, the heat's on around here," the vedette added solemnly.

I apologized with a nod and, signaling with a look toward the crowd that had formed at the tenement door, asked, intrigued, "So what's the story, Juana?"

Juana answered, "What's the story? Nothing, just that in this slum the black market's booming, and the cops are all up in arms. It's totally out in the open: red meat, leather goods, milk and butter, whatever. One of these days, they're going to bring in the cow through the front door. That's the story, my friend."

I got a knot in my throat and my previous smile stiffened from fear. In Cuba, killing a cow drew a severe penalty, even if it was your own property, and the black market in beef was as dangerous as the drug market in any other country. You got years, many years in jail, if you were caught violating the laws that protect those sacred cows.

Little by little, the near-riot had been calming down, the squad cars had left with their human cargo, and the mob had begun to disperse. The only one left was the mother of the twin traffickers, sobbing at the door of the tenement in the arms of a freckled, bald albino wearing wooden sandals, shorts, and a sleeveless shirt.

Out of nowhere, an officer appeared next to us, with a face that suggested he had few friends. He was one of those feckless peasants they bring in from the most remote mountains in Oriente who eventually earn the antipathy of the capital's natives. The habaneros, who are partiers and irreverent by nature, called these guys Palestinians. The little Chinese beautician remained as solemn as a statue of Sanfancón. The bells from a nearby church broke the silence and startled the little man, who immediately grabbed the singer's gloved arm.

"IDs, please," said the officer, extending his index finger like an earthworm.

His cold stare remained focused on the unique duo. Then he gave a once over to the weirdly shaped and heavy load I was carrying on my back. As each of us showed our ID, I ventured to inform him in a most cordial way, "*Compañero*, this is the famous Juana Bacallao."

But this Palestinian didn't utter a word and he took his time checking our papers.

"Well, it says here that her name is Nerys Amelia Martínez Salazar," he said.

Juana explained, "It's just that Juana Bacallao is my stage name, compañero…"

The officer cut her off. "Your stage name? And this little Chinese guy, he's what, a ballet dancer?" he added with disdain. Then, without allowing a response, he turned to me: "And you, what's the idea with the box? You got a dead body in there or what? C'mon, open up so we can see."

I thought the world was standing still around me. I got a cramp in my stomach, I broke into a cold sweat, and my ears went numb, producing an incredible pressure in my skull.

"Hey, did you hear me, or do we have a problem?" he said.

Juana looked at the ground, and I obeyed, holding the box horizontally in front of the man. The gendarme opened it slowly, looked the instrument up and down, furrowed his brow, made a face, and slammed down the lid; then he gave us back our papers, turned, and walked away, exclaiming, "Man, that horn stinks!"

As soon as the cop was out of sight, Juana whispered to me in a low voice, practically without moving her lips, "Andrés and Kemal got out of here just before the trouble started, so move your ass. None of this is about you."

Although my paranoia still didn't allow me to respond, I breathed a sigh of relief. I quickly said my goodbyes to the odd couple and continued on my way, getting as far away as possible from the troublesome tenement of El Trueno, walking towards Neptuno Street. When I got to the bus stop, I got lucky right away and a Route 43 bus came by, giving me a noisy ride all the way home to Marianao, on the other side of the world. It felt like I was escaping from hell with the Devil's trident hidden in my gig-bag.

When I got to my neighborhood, everything moved as if in slow motion. The spell was only broken by the sounds of an occasional Soviet military truck, the asthmatic sputtering of a 1940s gringo car, or the horrible rattle caused by my neighbor Tarzan's smoky, junky Czech motorcycle when he zoomed by, farting and spitting hot petrol. Tarzan was slender, brawny, and statuesque; he had tattoos, wore dark glasses, skin-tight sleeveless tops, ripped jeans, leather wristbands, and color-ful bandannas to hold his wild hair back.

The neighborhood kids admired him because he looked like the pirates in the movies they'd show on Sundays at the Cándido Cinema, and he seemed like Captain Hook himself on the broad and empty boulevard, cruising by on his rattling two-wheeler while the gleeful kids sang his praises from the sidewalks. Whenever Tarzan managed to get a few liters of fuel on the black market, the *rat-a-tat* of his motorcycle could be heard all over Marianao. It was like a war cry in that silent jungle, where the absence of electric juice during most of the day muted the radios, TVs, Chano the rock musician's electric guitar, and the Cándido movie theater itself.

The son-of-a-bitch bus driver (I realize this is a redundancy) drove past my stop and dropped me off on the corner, near the Cuesta Drugstore, next to what used to be the Ward Bakery, now turned into a residential home. It looked something like the Ringling Brothers circus trick with the overstuffed VW; it was almost impossible to imagine how they could get so many people into such little space. As I was going down my block on Forty-First Avenue, a little anti-aerodynamic Girón bus zoomed by, blowing a cloud of dust and blinding me for a few seconds. "Now I won't have to say hello to Lieutenant Mayedo and his repugnant wife if they're sitting on the porch," I thought.

My brains were practically boiling; when I got home, I had to hold onto the bronze door knocker on our big white-washed door. That's when I saw the note, written in pencil on a scrap of paper from a grocery bag (this was before we ran out of bags, paper, groceries, and everything else). The brief message was signed by none other than Dizzy Gillespie.

Ever since I was a kid I had heard fantastic stories about the legendary trumpet player, like the time he chased Cab Calloway with a switchblade all over the streets of New York, or the time he showed up for dinner at an upscale Buenos Aires restaurant on horseback, dressed like a gaucho from the Argentine pampas. Someone that unpredictable and eccentric was capable of anything, but the truth is that the message left on my door took me completely by surprise. It was written in some kind of Spanglish and more or less said, "*Hola*, Paquito, *Vine* lookin' for you, *pero no estabas*. See ya soon! Dizzy Gillespie."

I took the note from the door and took a good look around. Hmm, nothing, no one, absolute silence. "What the hell is this?" I thought, gazing at the paper somewhat incredulously. I couldn't explain such a letter, and I walked back out in the implacable sun toward the El Cedro Grocery, located on the corner by my house at Forty-First Avenue and Ninety-Fourth Street in Marianao.

My friend Pichilingo, a thin and mangy dog, was resting against the wall as always, scratching and licking his balls. Without stopping to greet him, I leapt up the three or four cracked concrete steps and past two faded pink columns. As had happened with every other private business at the beginning of the Revolution, El Cedro had been taken over by the government. As a result, the pauper shelves behind the mahogany counter, which had once boasted both domestic and imported products of all kinds, now displayed a combination of anti-American posters, empty bottles, moldy cans, and a large, frameless, cardboard-backed poster of our Maximum Leader. "Thanks, Fidel, for all the things you give us!" said the little hand-painted sign under the picture. To the left of it, the old freezer, with its dark wood and thick metal hinges, had been waiting years for a replacement part that could kickstart its exhausted gringo heart. There had once been a shelf above it painted a light green with gold and red stripes, where the fine liqueurs used to be, but it had fallen apart long ago. Hung from a rusty nail on the only shelf that still seemed solid, another sign signaled a prayer of sorts: *"Revolución es construir."*

I hadn't quite set foot inside the grocery when Jesús Cayón, the grocer, turned to me with a cynical little smile. "Did you get the note?" he asked.

Jesús was a good-natured peasant, fifty-ish, with a broad smile and a head of thinning gray hair. He loved to go for long sojourns into the countryside, get up at dawn to cut sugar cane at whatever plantation would have him in the faraway province of Camagüey. Zafra, or harvest season, was like a break for him. It seemed he used that incredibly tough work to escape the gossip on the block, the overflowing buses, the ever more frequent and longer blackouts, and the constant complaints from his customers about the eternal scarcity of basic products that never seemed to reach the neighborhood stores.

The furious roar of Tarzan's motorcycle brought me out of my revelry, and I said, "The ape man must have found some contraband fuel."

It was so hot the perspiration was rolling off my back in thick drops. I imagined Dizzy Gillespie in colorful swimming trunks, strolling around Varadero Beach, playing his horn while pointing to the sun and giving out Popsicles to refresh and delight everyone on the beach's steaming sand.

"Did I get the note?" I repeated the question.

Before I could answer myself, I realized that the customers in line with their ration cards to buy what few products the grocer had were all looking at me with a mixture of cynicism and curiosity. Sitting up high on the shoeshine chair as if he were on a king's throne was a very skinny man with reddish skin, wearing olive-green pants and a ragged undershirt that had once been white. A tight cap the same color as the pants gripped his head, as if it was trying by any means to control his messy, rebellious hair. In a slurry voice, from his wooden throne, the skinny guy asked, "Well, buddy, so… did you get the note?"

I nodded, trying to figure out what was going on, or at least what the joke was, and since the load on my back was pretty heavy, I put the little coffin on the floor, but only for a few seconds. Pichilingo, wagging his tail and sniffing what he hadn't laid eyes on in who knows how long, indiscreetly stuck his nose into it.

I made an inquisitive gesture to the neighborhood gossip queen, an old woman in her eternal and worn rubber flip-flops. Cheché was watching me from behind thick and smudged lenses that looked like they might collapse at any moment. The old woman had been head of the local Committee for the Defense of the Revolution since the day the government had created them; she'd been dedicated to watching the neighbors on our block and those surrounding ever since. But since Cheché was getting more deaf and blind by the day, she covered less territory and had less control now. A curtain of blue smoke emanated from the cigar stub she held in her toothless mouth and obscured her small, wrinkled face. The old lady just ignored me. She spit out something blackish from the side of her mouth.

Then it was Jesús the grocer who spoke from behind the counter: "There was a big black guy here looking for you, a real joker, talking nonsense and dressed like Sherlock Holmes."

The skinny guy in the shoeshine chair finished off the story while pretending to smoke a pipe: "Elementary, my dear Watson. He had on a plaid cape, tall boots, a double-billed hat, and he was even smoking the same kind of pipe that Sherlock smokes in the movies!"

Just then, Olga the mulatta was coming into the grocery store, all happy, swinging, and playful, immediately attracting lascivious looks and the envy of women.

"Yeah, and before he left, he started to puff on it to amuse Cachita la China's grandkids, and his cheeks blew up so big, they looked like they were going to explode!" said a honey-eyed voice behind my back. "Just like I'm telling you, music man… What a clown, that black guy!"

The grocer interjected: "Yeah, he was here with Arturo Sandoval, the trumpeter from Irakere. I don't know, but I don't think that guy's an American, and I think those two are up to something."

It was hard to imagine what a character like that was doing in such a remote neighborhood of Havana. There were no luxury hotels or stores that took dollars here. Foreigners never got this far out.

"Well, you be careful," Cheché warned. "Hanging out with foreigners isn't viewed too kindly by the Revolution, and you know that."

I didn't tell her to go to hell out of respect for her age, but it wasn't as if I didn't want to. Suddenly, we heard the insistent sound of a car horn and somebody calling my name out on the sidewalk. As I turned around, I could see an official car from the Ministry of the Interior with a driver at the wheel and an officer beside it, both dressed completely in olive green with guns at their waists.

The officer opened the back door of the gray mouse-like Soviet-made Volga.

"Get in," he said. "We need to have a chat."

He was tall, white, well built, with very black hair cut military-style, severe gestures, and a cutting tone in his voice. He was one of those guys who thought the whole world was Castro's military base. I could see the other guy, the driver, was a mulatto we described as *guayabú* in Cuba—big, fat-headed, with a faraway look. He was of a lower rank, with his round face bathed in sweat. An arm hung out of the window and a half-smoked cigar rested in his left hand.

"Who, me?" I asked.

"I told you, music man, whatever involves the black market and trafficking with foreigners is..."

But Cheché couldn't finish her ideological disquisition because she went into a coughing fit that doubled her over. "Maybe she'll just choke to death, the old snitch," I thought to myself, glad for once in my life for the tobacco industry.

"Yeah, you, the one with the little coffin on his shoulder," said the driver.

"Well, okay, but can I just drop off my instrument at my house?" I asked. "It'll be just a minute. May I?"

The officer outside the car answered with a wink. "Leave the what? No way, buddy. It's exactly what's in there that we're after." He came near and signaled toward the case, which I thought everyone but me assumed just carried an inoffensive saxophone. "It's heavy, isn't it?" he asked casually, gently tapping the box. I nodded sadly. Recovering his military cadence and taking me by the arm with authority he said, "Then let's go, it's getting late."

Resigned to the worst, I obeyed. Ashamed, and without looking back, I reluctantly climbed into the official car. The Volga's motor purred when turned on, and the smell of rubber and burnt grass already in the air became stronger. Without further explanations, my escorts started down Forty-First Avenue headed east, leaving a haze of yellow dust all over my neighborhood.

Pichilingo, the little dog, stopped scratching and licking long enough to chase and bark at the official car for a few meters. Tarzan greeted me warmly from his motorcycle as he went by, just as the neighbors came out to see how the police had taken away the musician. For dealing with foreigners? Trafficking in controlled merchandise? Illegal possession of dollars? Who knew! They would have to find out through the grapevine since that kind of thing hardly ever made it into *Granma*, the Communist Party's official newspaper. I dared to look out the car's back window, only to see old lady Cheché, still coughing, pointing at me, threatening with her index finger held high.

The two men kept their silence for the entire trip. They made a right turn on Thirty-First Avenue, and when they got to the corner with the defunct gas station, they turned up at the arrow that said "*Tropicana, un Paraíso Bajo las Estrellas*," toward the nightclub's gardens. As we made our way up the ramp to the most beautiful cabaret in the world, we could hear musicians practicing in the dressing rooms, camouflaged by the vegetation. A classic soprano was holding a very high note, which contrasted with the raspy beat that came from an African drum's thick skin.

We soon passed under the white arch flanked by willowy royal palms. Up ahead, next to the high iron fence, Rita Longa's delicately sculpted dancer greeted all visitors. Between the tangled forest trees, ivy, and exotic flowers the club's principal owner, Martin Fox, had brought from all over the world stood the famous fountain of muses by the Italian Aldo Gamba. According to legend, the sculptor, supposedly in a jealous rage, shot the young Englishwoman who was his model. He went to jail, where he carved the human-sized figures for that impressive fountain, which had first been part of the Casino Nacional. When the casino went under, Fox bought the fountain of muses, and when Gamba was released from prison, he married the pretty Englishwoman he'd tried to kill just a few years earlier.

That magical place was filled with history and ghosts from a past that was still close and fresh. With the fountain's waters whispering and the birds singing playfully on the tree branches, I let my mind wander and remembered hearing Armando Romeo's orchestra accompanying Rodney the Magician's fabulous productions. I imagined a fantastic chorus featuring the disparate voices of Olga Guillot, Nat King Cole, Carmen Miranda, Yma Sumac, Celia Cruz, Sara Vaughan, Bola de Nieve, Steve Allen, Benny Moré, Xiomara Alfaro, Paulina Álvarez, Desi Arnaz, Cab Calloway, Elena Burke, Trio Matamoros, Edith Piaf, Merceditas Valdés, and Pedro Vargas. I saw them making their entrances to the beat of Los Papines's drums, singing under the starry Cuban sky. Felo Bergaza's white piano emerged from a cloud of steam and colored bubbles on a revolving platform that went up and down. On top of it Lupe the ballet dancer executed an incredible pirouette.

The choral music in my head began to fade, along with the orchestra, the drums, the piano, and Felo Bergaza's sequins. The cloud, the lights, the colored bubbles all vanished as the official car slowed to a stop at the front door of the open-air club. The tall man got out, exchanged words with the militiaman in charge, and went in through the thick glass door.

I don't know if it was because of my paranoia, thirst, hunger, or the suffocating heat inside that car, but I started getting a very strong waft of raw meat. I put my left hand on the small coffin I'd placed on the back seat with me, afraid that those ten pounds of hidden beef would start to decompose and stink up a storm and that the lid on the whole Pandora's box would pop open.

What would it matter, though, if the police already knew everything and had knowingly taken me into custody with the goods on me? I wanted to confess and apologize but I didn't dare ask any questions my captors hadn't actually put to me, especially since I hadn't been formally arrested. "Get in, we need to have a chat," was all they had said. Although later they had added that what most interested them was what was in my case. That was worrisome. To what in my case were they referring, exactly? After all, it's not like the Cuban authorities are what we could call music fans. And what about all the other stuff I was carrying in the case that had been purchased on the black market?

To top it off, even that new sax had been lifted from the warehouse at the Ministry of Culture. I had traded mine for it, which was of lesser quality, by throwing in a few bucks. Some weeks later, when the instrument's disappearance was discovered, I had to take it apart, sand it down, and wash it with acid so it would look old and beat up and not be confused with the shiny new one they were looking for.

I realized the only legal things on me, in and out of the case, were the shirt I was wearing, which I'd gotten a few weeks before with my ration card, and my underwear, which my Aunt Josefa had sewn for me out of an old sheet we'd found in my grandmother's linen closet. What else was I carrying? A stolen sax, half an onion, a little bag of red beans, a piece of plantain, half a dozen garlic cloves, a bottle of Bebito cologne, and a medium size tube of Perla toothpaste... all illegal—my God!

There was no way I could explain where I'd gotten all that. In fact, the Wrangler jeans I was wearing had been sold to me by the cook at the Hotel Nacional, who'd stolen them from an Italian tourist. And there was also the mysterious note written by Dizzy Gillespie, a foreign musician.

"I'm screwed," I thought to myself, imagining the Count of Monte Cristo, Valeriano Weyler, and uric acid-poisoning red meats.

"Nothing can save me now," I muttered. "And to think how healthy it is to eat greens, fruits, and salads!"

My other self responded, a little louder, "Yeah, and where were you going to get the fruits and vegetables, you fool?"

The driver turned around and looked at me with sad, tired eyes and asked, "What did you say, compañero?"

"Nothing," I answered. "I was just saying that if it's this hot in April, we're going to roast in August."

The guy answered with a low groan as the other officer came back with a hurried step. He had a cigarette between his lips and a brown envelope in his hand when he jumped into the passenger seat next to the driver.

"To headquarters," he said dryly.

The driver started the engine immediately and sped out of the cabaret grounds. The word "headquarters" gave me a certain feeling of vertigo, and a strong desire to leap from that car and put an end once and for all to my delinquent lifestyle. But I didn't have the nerve. I had to relieve my suffering just sitting there, breathing in the warm and contaminated air coming in through the windows. I didn't even dare ask the officers for a smoke. It had been several days since I'd gone through the meager quota of cigarettes on my ration card, and I hadn't been able to get a single pack on the black market.

After going around the outskirts of the city for what seemed a thousand times, the official car finally arrived at the front gate of the most sinister, sordid, and feared place on the whole island: Villa Maristas, the general headquarters for the notorious State Security apparatus.

That's when I was really sorry I hadn't leapt from the car. The name of that solemn place—Marist Village, in English—came about because, prior to the communist takeover, the campus belonged to a school run by the Marist brothers. The stories about what went on inside those walls made Bela Lugosi's horror pictures look like Donald Duck and Frankenstein's monster like Little Red Riding Hood.

"Damn, this is happening to me for being such a glutton," I lamented when I found myself sitting in a small, white-walled room where there was only a dark wooden table, two chairs, a metal ashtray, a phone, and my ridiculous sax case between my legs, which were trembling now from cold and fear. The A/C was on full blast. About fifteen minutes after I got there, a uniformed woman came in without saying a word and left a metal jar of ice water and two glasses on the table. Seconds later, the higher-ranking of the two officers who had brought me came in. He still had the brown envelope he'd picked up at the Tropicana in his hand. He poured water into the two glasses and offered me one.

"Well, we're certainly cooler here than out there, aren't we?" he said.

He sat down at the table in front of me, took out a pack of export-only H. Upmanns from his shirt pocket, opened it, offered me one, put one to his own lips, then pulled out a lighter and lit both. We smoked in silence for a few minutes. I thought I heard thuds in the distance and the muffled cry of someone they were trying to gag. A shiver went up my spine, but I didn't say peep. The man ignored the terrifying sounds, moved to the empty chair, brought it closer to the table, and laid out some photos he took from the brown envelope.

"Do you know these people?" he asked.

He pointed to a picture of a very made-up Japanese dancer with ornaments in her hair, a raised leg, and a fan in each hand. I tried to take a good look but explained that, with all that makeup, it was really hard to identify anybody.

"How about this one?"

"Ah, that's Juana Bacallao," I said.

Pointing to a black man topped by a Turkish fez and wearing a typical African dashiki that reached the floor, the diplomat was bowing slightly toward Juana, who had her hands in the air, exhibiting yet another of her theatrical poses.

The officer continued: "With the ambassador of Ghana, at the entrance to the Hotel Capri, and that's her beautician."

I recognized him as soon as he showed me a photo of the little Chinese guy who had been with the vedette that very afternoon.

The partisan continued in a scolding tone: "Well, that's the same Chinese faggot from the first photo I showed you. He organizes little parties where fags go and dress up as 'artists,' but they're going to get it, because quite a few tourists and even diplomats from socialist countries are going to these so called 'artist' events. What do you think about that?"

He paused as he sucked on his cigar before grinding it down in a rage in the nearby ashtray. I didn't know what to say, so I put mine out too in the same ashtray already loaded with the malodorous remains of previous interrogations. Now the room was filled with a sticky fog, the air we breathed had been contaminated, and the mood had turned suffocating.

The man motioned for me to come closer to the table, and he did the same. I got a whiff of my interrogator's thick, nicotine-laced breath, and I imagined that mine didn't smell much better. How badly I wanted to rid myself of that nasty habit!

"Everybody here knows that trafficking in meat, and especially with foreigners, is a no-go, you understand me? Unless, of course, it's been approved from higher up."

He was calmer when he finished but continued to take photos out of the brown envelope, laying them on the table.

This time he stayed quiet and watched as I looked dumb-founded at the image of that unique, unquestionable character whose image was captured in the instant photo. He was actually a bit on the thick side, dark-skinned, you could see a plush goatee without a moustache around the broad grin. Perched on his flat nose and wide nostrils was a pair of thick-framed glasses. He was wearing riding pants and boots, a plaid cape, and a double-billed hat of the same material. One hand held his singular trumpet, the other a gigantic ivory pipe.

Tentatively lifting my eyes and fully aware I was still carrying the note that had mysteriously appeared on my front door, I dared to ask, "Compañero, are you trying to tell me that Dizzy Gillespie is mixed up with orgies and illegal parties here in Cuba?"

The interrogator continued: "I have nothing to say about that, and in fact perhaps you know the answer to that better than me, because you know these citizens who are having strange interactions with foreigners, and then there's that Yankee musician who got off a boat asking about you. Arturo Sandoval picked him up at the pier in his green 1956 Opel and took him straight to your house in Marianao, where we picked you up. Isn't that right?"

My stomach was doing flips and my head was about to explode. I couldn't for the life of me figure out the relationship between Juana Bacallao, the little Chinese transvestite, and the famous American trumpet player looking all over Havana for me in Sandoval's old beat-up Opel automobile. The thuds and muffled cries had stopped and now there was just an uncomfortable silence, which I filled with mental strategies on how I was going to confess my "beeficide" and the provenance of all the other things I had on me. I would then honestly and sincerely deny and reject any implications of homosexuality, as well as any personal links to Dizzy Gillespie or any other American musician.

I began to explain with my eyes firmly focused on the black box between my legs: "Look, compañero, there are many capitalist temptations, gluttony…"

But at that moment, the phone that had been a silent witness on the table suddenly began to ring. I jerked, startled, and the man, who had been staring at me until that very moment, held his palm up for me to stop talking and picked up the receiver.

"Yes," he said, and poised himself to listen, furrow-browed, his eyes moving from my face to my instrument case and back. "Well, there's no question about it, we'll have to take him back right away."

That's all he said before he hung up, stood, turned around, and stormed out without saying goodbye.

On the table, next to the photo of Gillespie and the others, there was one of Yudislexis, the chubby girl from the diner, wearing a bikini and dancing with a couple of young guys, also wearing very little, who were none other than Plácido and Domingo, the twin traffickers (not exactly saints) from El Trueno. Nearby, wearing a feathered turban and what looked like women's panties with lace and everything, Kemal Kairuz was playing the piano.

On either side of the Arab, Juana Bacallao and a Japanese geisha were singing a duet. It was possible to distinguish Andrés Castro and his son in the background, both dressed like hunters and playing their trumpets. Next to them, with a diplomatic air about him, was the African guy from the previous photo.

"We're all going to go up in flames; the only one missing from the photos is me—not that they need the evidence, considering all I'm carrying on me," I worried.

The fat driver who'd brought us opened the door and ordered, "Grab your little horn, we're leaving."

I could hear a woman sobbing on the other side of the wall and the echo of a masculine voice whose words I couldn't make out. I threw the heavy case on my shoulder and followed him to a poorly-lit hallway that was long and narrow and had many doors. Fully-uniformed men and women kept coming in and out of the doors. Voices giving commands, and faraway, indecipherable noises could be heard from everywhere.

Avoiding everyone without a single greeting, the driver led the way. His right hand rested on the handle of the gun at his waist. I could see the salt stains from dried sweat on the back and shoulders of his military uniform. He had a just-lit Cohiba in his mouth, which, with his heavy but quick step, made him look like a crazed locomotive on invisible tracks, pulling a solitary car, which was me.

A blinding sun overwhelmed me when we finally got outside. I couldn't see a thing as I climbed in the backseat of the car, which took off like a wild stallion, leaping over flooded potholes in the tired streets of my beloved and impoverished native city. At the time, I was too confused to know if I was happy, sad, or just a little scared, but I was certainly relieved to have walked out unscathed from that terrible place, filled with smoke and ash and those heart-wrenching screams.

I was glad to be sweating again. Now the carbon monoxide from the buses blended with the smell of burnt oil from the heavy Soviet trucks and those old, invincible American cars seemed like Chanel No. 5 to me. I felt like I was swimming in sweet freedom, even if only halfway.

We went by Ciudad Deportiva and its fountain, which had been lit in other times. It had been inaugurated during the presidency of Dr. Ramón Grau San Martín, a lifelong bachelor who named his sister-in-law, Paulina Ansina, as the First Lady of the republic. When the fountain was completed, the habaneros, as jocular as always, called the thing "Paulina's Bidet." I laughed a little, remembering the amusing way my Aunt Josefa told stories, and all the gossip about Grau and his sister-in-law.

The car went by the Surgical Hospital, over the railroad tracks, crossed Cerro and continued down Twenty-Sixth Street. In front of the zoo, there was still the Barbarám Club, in the same building where Bola de Nieve, the great chansonnier used to live.

The Volga continued its flight, ignoring lights and traffic signs. That man drove like a maniac, but there finally came a moment when I was so exhausted, physically and mentally, that I fell asleep, though I don't know for how long, with my head on the hard little coffin that Romanian Jewish kid had made for me.

I dreamt I was in New York's famous Birdland Club. Sherlock Holmes was next to me, playing on a gigantic pipe that looked like a saxophone, and I was Dizzy Gillespie, blowing on my crooked horn. Kemal Kairuz was practically naked, seated at the piano and wearing his feathered turban, and

Juana Bacallao was really Ella Fitzgerald, wearing a metal-green wig and dressed like a member of the militia. Andrés and Andresito Castro, decked out as hunters with Bermuda shorts and safari helmets, played trumpets made of meat, and standing between the two of them, the Ghanaian ambassador was slapping a giant batá drum he held between his powerful legs.

The club, called El Cedro, like the grocery store in my neighborhood, was decorated with dusty, broken shelves, a beat-up shoeshine stand, and long rows of empty bottles and rusty cans. At a table by the bandstand, chubby Yudislexis wore a daring dotted bikini and hung sweetly off her beau, Mongo Mandarria. In a dark and lonely corner, the driver of the official car was passionately making out with his tall, handsome superior, whose right hand had vanished into the other's fly.

"Mother of God, I can't believe this!" I thought, stunned.

In the most animated part of the cabaret were the twins, Plácido and Domingo Calzadilla, accompanied by their father, Ramón, the operatic tenor, and the Chinese beautician (the first looking like a Pinkerton guard and the second like Madame Butterfly's Cio Cio San). Contrasting with the rustic environs, there was a crystal bar, filled with gleaming glasses and colorful bottles. The bartender was Dracula, sipping on a Bloody Mary between clients. At the shadowy front door, Cheché's always-vigilant silhouette could be seen, alert.

"Mantecaaaa!" yelled Jesús the grocer from the audience, lifting his arm in the air to make the request and drawing approving hoots from the crowd.

Sherlock Holmes got the message, counted off, and the rhythm section began to vamp on the intro to Chano Pozo's famous piece. A loud noise from Tarzan's motorcycle could be heard from outside, incapable of adapting itself to bebop's more angular beats. The music was building toward a crescendo, the rhythm increasing in excitement, and just about when I was going to solo, I woke shaking from my dream, with a sudden halt and the sound of something heavy falling.

We had arrived at our destination, and the military guys opened the back door of the car without warning. The sax case I was using as a pillow fell to the ground in the underground parking lot where we'd come to a stop. Instinctively, I held on to the car door so that I wouldn't follow the case down to the ground, where it had hit hard enough to pop open with its criminal contents.

The fat driver ordered me out. I immediately obeyed, and after closing the lid and throwing the little coffin over my shoulder, I let myself be taken down various service hallways, which I soon recognized as the back of the kitchen at the Habana Libre, the old Hilton Hotel. We finally went through a side door that led to the dressing rooms, which were so familiar to me. They smelled of cheap perfume, coffee, cold beer, and sweaty rumba dancers. In other words, they smelled like a nightclub, a cabaret, a fragrance I'd loved since the cradle. The tall man opened one of the rooms and began to say something, but I interrupted him to tell him that my father used to work there many years back with Fernando Mulens's orchestra, and that I felt totally at home. The two officers looked at each other and shrugged.

It was obvious that the name of Matanzas's great composer meant nothing to these guys. With the same tendency I've always had toward daydreaming, I started thinking about years before, as if I were watching the elegant, kind figure cut by Mulens conducting from the piano bench. There was my father on sax and a young Juan Formell playing bass with the house band.

The driver's voice brought me back to the present: "Okay then, after you get your horn ready, come out to the cabaret stage, where they're waiting for you. You must play in the name of the Revolution, to sing high its praises. We have to beat imperialism at its own game. And hurry up, you're late."

"Late for what, compañero?"

I asked in vain, since both officers merely saluted and turned, exiting through the same service door by which we'd come in.

I put the little coffin down on the long table in front of the makeup mirrors and tried to put my instrument together while trying to figure out what the hell to do with the meat, the onion half, and the garlic I had stuffed in the bell of the saxophone—not to mention the piece of plantain, the bag of red beans, Gillespie's mysterious note, the bottle of Bebito cologne, and the tube of Perla toothpaste I had in my stolen blue jeans.

Then I heard a voice behind me say, "It'd be best if we put that in the bar's fridge." My fear totally exhausted by that point, I calmly turned and saw none other than Kemal Kairuz, without his turban but rather in a suit and tie. "Unless you want that meat to spoil."

In the distance we could hear the improbable and distinctive sound of Stan Getz's tenor. Looking both ways out in the hallway, Kemal opened the red bag with Arabic lettering that I'd made fun of hours before in front of his building on Ánimas Street.

"I work here at the piano bar," he said with a shrug. "You know, I don't think you have any choice but to trust me on this. If you want to give me the key to your house, I can drop this off. I have to go get some music at Tropicana, and Tarzan is going to drop me off on his motorcycle since he's going that way anyway. It's no big deal for me to stick this in your fridge. So just tell me what you want to do."

As I put everything in the bag and handed him the key to my house in Marianao, suspicious though grateful, I asked, "Why would you take such a risk for me, Kemal?"

Without looking at me, he took his time to answer. "Oh, you know, the fag in me." He laughed, turned, and flew down the cabaret's hallway. "I'll leave the key with your neighbor Carmita!" he said with a wave of the hand.

Getz's beautiful phrases were filling the air, and, having this huge load lifted off my shoulders, I got back to putting my instrument together and started down the same hallway by which the Arab pianist had just left, and from which the intriguing sounds were emanating. I could never have imagined that hallway would take me to such an incredible musical encounter with artists I'd admired since childhood. Everything seemed like a hallucinatory and fantastic dream.

The thing was that, inexplicably, Dizzy Gillespie, Stan Getz, Earl Hines, and David Amram had all shown up on a cruise ship that day in Havana Bay. There had been nothing in the mass media about it, and there wasn't a musician on the island who had a clue about the valuable cargo on that ship— except Arturo Sandoval, who ran into Dizzy Gillespie as he casually walked by and heard him mention my name. I later heard that Mario Bauzá, an old friend of my father's, had told him about me. All of a sudden, and under orders from who knows who, that jam session was organized that afternoon at the Habana Libre's Caribe cabaret, with American and Cuban musicians going at it. Later that night, there was a surprisingly joyous concert at the Teatro Mella

As it turned out, the hotel was simultaneously hosting a gathering of seniors celebrating fifty years in the sugar industry, and who knows what sick mind decided to punish them, making them go to our hours-long jazz concert at the Mella, while legions of genuine jazz fans and musicians were kept out.

Naturally, State Security blocked access to the theater where the Americans were playing about two hours before the show, and they didn't let anyone in who wasn't authorized from higher up or couldn't show an ID saying they'd been in the sugar industry for fifty years. Is that magic realism or what?

For those of us lucky ones who were able to take part in the historic event, it was a beautiful experience, since we got to play alongside musicians we knew and admired until then only from recordings—Rudy Rutherford, Ron Mc-Clure, Billy Hart, Ray Mantilla, John Ore, Mickey Roker, Ben Brown, Joanne Brackeen, and Rodney Jones. When they got back to New York, the journalist Arnold Jay Smith and the American musicians told Bruce Lundvall, then the president of CBS Records, what they'd seen in Havana. This made him so interested in us that he brought the whole group to the United States the following year. We came with Irakere to record for CBS, and even George Wein, the famous producer of the Kool Jazz Festival at Carnegie Hall, included us in the lineup. The night's stars were the piano duo of Bill Evans and McCoy Tyner.

At the end of our set at Carnegie Hall (which we played against the express wishes of the Cuba security agents detail accompanying us), we were joined on stage by David Amram, Maynard Ferguson, Stan Getz, and the ineffable Dizzy Gillespie, with his broad and mischievous grin, clowning around, inflating his cheeks, and… with his plaid cape, high boots, double-billed cap, and the pipe in his mouth just like the one Sherlock smoked in the movies! Just exactly like that windy, sunny April afternoon in the grocery owned by the peasant Jesús Cayón, back in my old Havana neighborhood.

All Aboard!

Yeyito, you have probably already imagined that another powerful reason why I love this career is all the traveling. Even if airplanes aren't my favorite, I love the idea of moving back and forth!

Don't you like traveling, Yeyo? I just love it, and before my first international trip, I had been traveling with my family all around Cuba. Since my grandfather Lino was a veteran of our War of Independence against Spain, my dad used to take us to visit General Antonio Maceo's mausoleum every December 7 at Cacahual, near the town of Punta Brava. On that date in 1896, Maceo (The Bronze Titan) was wounded and died, next to his assistant Panchito Gómez Toro, son of General Máximo Gómez. Actually, the first time we traveled far from Havana was on that thirteen-hour train ride to visit my mother's family in the city where she was born: Santiago de Cuba, in the Oriente province. Besides me, the rest of the excursionists were my brother Enrique, my mom, and my aunt Muña. Our cousin Evencia was waiting for us at the Santiago train station.

Although the city that encircles the bay of Santiago in the southeast of the island is surrounded by mountains, it's very hot there. Oriente is where the most delicious fruits in

Cuba are grown. As Félix B. Caignet said in his song, "Caney de Oriente is the land of love, where God's hands spread his blessings and where fruits are just like flowers, well perfumed and glutted in honey..."

It was there in the Caney Mountains where my grandmother Panchita was born, of a Spanish father and an aboriginal mother, one of the few that survived the Spanish colonization. My mother used to tell me that Panchita's father was a Galician, even more brutish than a mule. He never registered his daughters, nor did he send them to school; learning to read and write was a thing for men. According to him, women should stay home until some fool turns up, marries them, takes them away, and the cycle begins again.

We still have some pictures of that trip, taken at the "Loma del Viso" commemorating the day that "gringos" came to Santiago during the Spanish-American War. Then my aunt Muña, who was very emotional, wanted to pray to la Caridad del Cobre (Our Lady of Charity), patron saint of Cuba at her church in El Cobre, a tiny town at the entrance of Santiago surrounded by the Sierra Maestra Mountains. While Muña said many Lord's Prayers and Hail Marys, my brother and I chased a goat outside the church.

Muña ran out of prayers, the goat ran far from our reach, and our *santiaguera* cousin proposed to visit the Bacardí Museum; a huge, very European, impressive building, where there was a mummy straight from Egypt on display. There were also a few relics that belong to Antonio Maceo. I never understood what the "mummy" had to do with Maceo and I didn't dare ask either, probably not to sound ignorant... who knows!

Years later in Miami, I met a grandson of Don Emilio Bacardí, and he told me that his grandfather had purchased the mummy on a tourist trip to Cairo. When they landed in Cuba, his grandfather, slipping a bill under the table, told the customs officer, "C'mon man, be reasonable, we're not going to argue over a few pounds of dried meat, right?"

The officer looked around and, placing the bill in his pocket, wrote something in the customs declaration, stamped it, kept the original in a drawer and gave a copy to Mr. Bacardí. It said, "jerked beef for personal use."

About an hour later we said goodbye to the mummy, and my mother bought some flowers that we placed on José Martí's grave, in the name of my grandfather Lino, the veteran. We habaneros never came to terms with the fact that José Martí, the most illustrious Cuban, who was born on Paula Street in Havana, on January 28, 1853, is buried at the Santa Ifigenia cemetery in Santiago de Cuba. Even more contradictory is the fact that Antonio Maceo, born in Santiago de Cuba, rests at Punta Brava, in the Havana province. It's a Cuban thing!

Almost four decades later I learned that the great contrabass player and composer Israel "Cachao" López was born in the same house on Calle de Paula and that every January 28, they would empty the house so that children for schools could visit the birthplace of our "National Poet."

You can't say you visited Santiago unless you go by Padre Pico Street, where you find stairs so high they touch the sky. At least that's what I thought in those days when I was a child. Afterwards we visited my mother's cousin, the sweet and loving Juanica, who lived in the Altamira neighborhood. We went all over Santiago and up Enramada Street to the center of the city, where Carlos Manuel de Céspedes Park is located, along with the Casa Granda Hotel and the home-cum-museum of Diego Velázquez, first colonial governor of the island when Santiago was its capital.

From far away, mixed with sparrows singing and palm trees swaying, you could hear the guitars and voices of Santiago's legendary troubadours, drinking, making music, and having a good time at Céspedes Park.

Since it was getting hotter by the minute and we were exhausted, we sat in a small outdoor bar to drink Pru Oriental, a refreshing drink made out of roots from the area. A while later, a fat lady in an odalisque costume turned around the corner playing a lyre like Nero's. My brother had a fit of giggles, because right around that time Disney's *Fantasia* was playing and the lady resembled a ballerina hippopotamus from the film. Behind her, a man dressed as a magician ate light bulbs and other glass objects. He then passed an old hat so people would put money in it. The strange pair finally got to our table, and my aunt Muña, who was quite witty, sized the magician and his fat lady up and said, "What about if after I finish my pru I eat the glass and keep the hat with everything in it?"

Dropping her jaw from the surprise, the fat lady opened her eyes wide like an owl, and the man had no other choice than to laugh out loud and walk away with his human hippopotamus.

Years later, I went with Manolito "Calandraca" Armesto, a photographer and bongo player, to the Rancho Luna Bar on Twenty-Third Street and Paseo to have a beer... Do you remember it? Or did you never get to Havana, Yeyo? There we met an unusual, soft-spoken character who approached customers with an odd proposition: "If you buy me beer, when I finish I will eat the glass, except for the bottom because it's too hard."

I guess swallowing glass objects is a psychosomatic condition (a sort of goat or shark complex, perhaps), because on another occasion Carlo Emilio Morales, the guitar player from Irakere, told me that while on tour with the group in Santa Clara (Las Villas Province), they found a kind of crazy guy that ate light bulbs, milk bottles, and razorblades. On any Miami radio station, where even hurricanes and the sex aberrations among birds are political, they would have said they were eating glass because of how hungry people are in Cuba.

My first trip abroad happened in 1957. To appear on national television in the Dominican Republic for several weeks was unheard of for a nine-year-old boy and quite exciting. You see, Yeyito, I was like a child with a new toy, the new toy being my brand new career as an international musician.

I remember my dad was even more nervous than me. The Valdivia Sisters Quartet was flying with us. We boarded a Delta flight that made one stop at the tiny Port Au Prince airport in the neighboring Republic of Haiti, the first independent country in the New World (an example of how independence doesn't always mean freedom, much less progress). We were there a couple of hours confronting the very unfriendly and mistrusting looks of François Duvalier's soldiers, who were armed to the teeth. We finally took off to the Dominican capital. The dictator had changed Santo Domingo's name and called it Ciudad Trujillo. What an excessive ego, that of Rafael Leónidas Trujillo Molina, the asshole that made people call him "Generalísimo," Benefactor, and Father of the New Mother Land. All that grandiloquence, and behind his back people would call him "Chapitas" for all the medals, won in imaginary combats, that he wore on his ridiculous Napoleonic suits.

It's rained a lot since that trip to Santiago de Cuba with my aunt and my mother, and after Santo Domingo perspective on life was never the same.

But don't think that through my travels around the world everyone I met was as regrettable as the Dominican dictator. I've also bumped into cool and interesting people like the glass eaters and the fat odalisque I mentioned earlier.

A few years back, pianist Ahmad Jamal and I coincided in a concert tour of Thailand, along with Chris Botti, Kenny G, Regina Carter, Nancy Wilson, and Dizzy Gillespie's orchestra, which I directed then. Jamal, one of Miles Davis's favorite pianists, whose birth name is Freddy "Fritz" Jones, was coming back with his trio from the other side of the world. It had been a long tour, and he was very tired. On top of that, with the World Trade Center tragedy and his Arabic name, they delayed him even more at airports with questions and searches. "I already play for free, Paquito," he would say, half joking and half serious. "I just charge to get to the gig."

By now you've probably heard of the Kingdom of Thailand, Yeyito. It's a very interesting, picturesque Southeast Asian country. It's adjacent to Laos and Cambodia to the east, the Gulf of Thailand and Malaysia to the south, and the Andaman Sea and Burma to the west. The country was previously known as Siam. They changed its name for the first time in 1939 to Prathet Thai, then because it was reverted during World War II, they changed it back again in 1949.

"Prathet" means "country," and the word "thai" means "free" or "freedom" in the language of Thailand. The word also describes their ethnic majority. This group obtained their freedom over two millennia ago, upon their escape from the Chinese and arrival at this region. So even though Prathet Thai translates literally as "country of free people" in English it became Thailand (land of the Thai).

Among other activities, their King, Bhumibol Adulyadej, plays the saxophone. He loves jazz, and when he was younger he used to jam with Benny Goodman, James Moody, and other famous musicians of the genre. The personality cult in that exotic land is taken to its maximum expression. There are two or three huge pictures of the monarch on every block, and I'm not exaggerating.

There are elephants all over the place, and there's even a park in Bangkok where they (the elephants) play football, dance, play drums, and paint pictures.

When we got to the Suvarnabhumi Airport in Bangkok on that Thailand tour, a great surprise awaited: our dear friend Jacques Muyal. We had met him through Dizzy Gillespie in Switzerland, his adopted country. Jacques is Jewish, born in Tangier, North Africa, when it was a very prosperous international territory, Muyal tells us. During the 1950s, the Voice of America (VOA) kept two ships in the Atlantic re-transmitting their programs from Washington to Europe and Africa. There, with the extraordinary view of the Strait of Gibraltar that unites the Atlantic with the Mediterranean, Jacques Muyal, at age fifteen and sixteen, associated with VOA and conducted a jazz program on International Tangier Radio. During those years he became friends with Dizzy Gillespie, Patato Valdés, Herbie Mann, José Mangual, Randy Weston, and many other American musicians that toured the area with sponsorship from the Department of State. Years later, Jacques Muyal became an engineer and was one of the developers of the handmade NAGRA tape recorders in Switzerland. NAGRA tape recorders were most popular in the movie industry.

Due to racial segregation and other abuses to the black community in the United States, Afro-American musicians sometimes mistrust and reject white people they don't know well. Dizzy Gillespie was totally the opposite. He always struggled against racial differences. Jacques tells us that once Dizzy and Max Roach were lunching in an outdoors restaurant and he noticed the drummer kept a distance, showing contempt. All he spoke about was Africa—Africa here, Africa there, Africans this or that—until Jacques got impatient and said: "Look here, Max. No more nonsense talk. If you want to talk Africa, the only real African at this table is me! Okay?"

Well, the whole thing ended with Dizzy laughing out loud, a tight handshake and a friendship that lasted until Max Roach's death. Since then, and since the man had adopted a Swiss nationality, we called Jacques Muyal the "Afro-Swiss." A unique and endearing friend, the only thing he lacks to be a musician is to play an instrument. Small detail, isn't it, Yeyito?

But Jacques Muyal is not the only one. Throughout my long career, I have confirmed that people exist who, even though they do not play a musical instrument, have become an integral part of our international music community because of their love and dedication to this art form. This is the case with

Dr. Cristóbal Díaz Ayala: Cuban by birth, resident of Puerto Rico, attorney by profession. A man of enterprise and writer on musical subjects, he has published a substantial amount of reference books for those who study Latin American music today. I asked "Uncle Toby" (a nickname used by those who love him) to write something for this book. So here it is, a tender vignette by Cristóbal Díaz Ayala:

Many years ago I was at a musician's party in La Guaira, Venezuela. A musician who resembled our dear "Gallego" of Los Guaracheros de Oriente arrived. He was short, chubby, and spontaneous, just like Gallego. We were introduced, and he told me that he was a founder of Sonero Clásico del Caribe.

I mentioned I admired the group a great deal, mainly because of their love and loyalty to the Cuban "Son." He then explained that ever since he was a boy he liked Cuban music and had always played it, because he wanted to know more about it.

"I had a great book about Cuban music," he said. "But I loaned it out and lost it. I really miss it too."

Thinking it was a book by Alejo Carpentier or Argeliers León, I mentioned both, but they weren't it. I asked, "Could it be Musica Cubana del Areito a la Nueva Trova?*"*

"That's it!" he said.

When I said I was the author, he hugged me and told me the story of his life. We both forgot there were other guests in the room, and he bombarded me with questions. We made a date for the following afternoon at three o'clock in my hotel, where I would give him a copy of the book he had lost. When he finally got there at six o'clock, the poor guy was all sweaty and breathless. He explained that he was so late because he brought me copies of several Sonero Clásico del Caribe albums that I didn't have. He also brought me a set of maracas he made himself. Besides being a musician, he also built Cuban musical instruments that were very popular in Venezuela.

My new friend's name was Carlos Emilio Landaeta, better known as "Pan con Queso" (Bread and Cheese), director of the aforementioned group, who from a very young age specialized in all Cuban percussion instruments. He told me that when he started playing he was so young that when offered a drink, he would say, "Better bring me some bread and cheese," thus the nickname. He was related to Maestro Landaeta, creator of the almost national anthem of Venezuela: "Alma Llanera."

Unfortunately our friendship didn't last long, since my dear, eloquent friend died two or three years later. During my next trip to Caracas I visited his grave with his widow. He lives in the best-located cemetery I have seen in my life, over a terrace on one of the many mountains that surround his beloved city. "Pan con Queso" has Caracas at his feet. He can glance through it with the eyes of the spirit right from his watchtower whenever he wants to.

Yeyito, I suppose you have already found people on your path that have worked for a long time in theaters or something related to scenic arts, music, or the like, but never learned a thing.

My good friend, the Mexican sculptor Carlos Aguilar y Linares, telephoned Mexico City's Bellas Artes Theater to ask for the exact date and time of my quintet's presentation with Brenda Feliciano and the Symphonic Orchestra of Mexico. The program was a sort of tribute to the music of George Gershwin and Ernesto Lecuona, who is considered by some (although not me) the Cuban Gershwin. The orchestra would be conducted by Carlos Miguel Prieto, its actual director. The woman who answered the telephone asked Carlos to wait a "little bit" (*tantito*) while she located the information. After a while she came back and said, "Mr. Aguilar, there is nothing for Saturday with Mr. Paquito D'Rivera. The ones announced are Gershwin and Lecuona, and although I don't know much about 'jak' (meaning jazz), these gentlemen must be very popular, because we're almost sold out."

My friend Carlos didn't even bother to clarify the situation, and, holding in his laughter, he reserved two of the available seats to take his wife to see George Gershwin and Ernesto Lecuona at Mexico City's magnificent Bellas Artes Theater.

A Musician's Thing

Going back to your question of whether it's worth it to pursue a music career, Yeyo, let me tell you what the great American sax player Phil Woods said to a group of students. "You cannot even imagine what a musician's life is like on the road until you do what we call 'One-Nighters' for at least a year," he said.

Music schools should demand a certain final exam from their students in order to test if they really have the natural talent, stamina, and perseverance necessary for this profession. The test Mr. Woods recommends is sort of a simulator of a one-year-long tour, and it works more or less as follows:

A school bus is parked at a given point of a very large track and field stadium, opposite to where the bandstand is, some two hundred to three hundred meters away.

The event is supposed to start at eight o'clock, but you guys arrive by yourselves at around three o'clock for sound check. You're wearing your tuxedos already, because dressing rooms have been reserved just for the high-ranking politicians in attendance, not for musicians. Then you do the setup, check the microphones, look (unsuccessfully, of course) for a good reed, put the book in order, and all that stuff. Then, suddenly, technical difficulties emerge, and it takes an hour and a half for the sound guys to solve the annoying feedback that has been harassing you all that time.

Finally they fix the problem, but then, as per union regulations, sound check abruptly ends at five. For security reasons, nobody is allowed to enter the arena's building or to go out of the track area. So you have to wander around that sport field for three hours. Then, when show time is approaching, you start walking towards the stage. Suddenly, dark clouds are covering the sky, and ten minutes before eight o'clock rain starts to come down aggressively. You have to grab your instrument and the book and run to the bus, parked three hundred meters away.

Then the rain stops and after taking your places on the stage, you enthusiastically get prepared to play the fantastic jazz suite you have rehearsed ad infinitum for such an important occasion. However, what you are asked to play instead is "The Star-Spangled Banner." After that, the politicians spend so much time talking about their plans for the future that there is no time left to play anything other than a John Phillip Souza March as a kind of bowl music while the politicians exit, talking animatedly among themselves.

Almost immediately, the road manager urges you guys to board the bus as soon as possible and hit the road for the long ride ahead. No time or place for shower, sit-down supper, or anything of the sort. As you reach the bus, three hundred meters away, the driver hands everyone a hot dog and soda, announcing that *musicians* are not included in the banquet offered by the university *music* department. Then you eat your hot dog, drink your root beer, and get prepared to go around the track and field camp a thousand, two thousand, or even three thousand times.

Yet you are happy, knowing that the next gig is in a jazz club, so you'll be able to play that fantastic jazz suite that you guys have rehearsed ad infinitum. What you don't suspect is that the club is so small you'll have to fit your big band on a tiny stage more suitable for a guitar and piccolo duet, that after playing the three seventy-five-minute sets required by the owner on Fridays and Saturdays, you have to share your room with three more cats, and all they want to do is to practice their damned horns all night long. And how about the bread (if any)? Hmmm! We better not even talk about that.

So you do that kind of traveling-playing-feeding 365 times in similar settings to complete your studies on what it is like to be a whole year of working as a musician on extreme road conditions. If you survive, and if at the end of this "tor-touring" simulation you still have any desire to play music, then you will go for a brief psychiatric test, join the union, and... welcome to the club!

Phil Woods is a very articulate, skeptical man. He has publicly confessed he doesn't consider himself a jazz innovator—although he's been undoubtedly one of the most influential saxophonists in the history of jazz, a history in which there are plenty saxophonists. Sometimes the topic of "supposed originality" is exaggerated and taken to extremes. The tendency seems to be to underestimate those who (supposedly) have not achieved a more or less distinguishable voice. To accomplish a voice of your own is neither easy nor necessary. If it were (and maybe I'm exaggerating), we'd only have two or three jazz groups in the country.

Brazilian musician Cláudio Roditi told me once that he thought honesty was much more important than the obsession jazz people have with originality. "Play what you feel and to hell with everyone else!" he said. Mind you, this was someone who with the passing of time has become one of the most identifiable contemporary trumpet players.

The one and only Tito Puente, a greatly imitated artist, used to say, "I only wanted to be accepted among Afro-Cuban jazz people," and although Tito's idols were Machito and Mario Bauzá, he undisputedly became part of history as a true icon of Latin music—just like Jon Faddis, who, from being sort of a copy of Dizzy Gillespie, achieved a very personal "virtuosisimo" style. In fact, Dizzy himself, who began by imitating his idol Roy Eldridge, almost unconsciously turned into an "American Original"—sort of a Cadillac of American culture, something Eldridge never even aspired to become.

I remember a funny story I read about a guy who tried to reproach Phil Woods for spending a lifetime trying to copy Charlie Parker. Phil, witty as ever, handed the guy his alto saxophone and answered, "Okay, I agree. Now *you* try to imitate Charlie Parker, asshole."

As with all human beings, sometimes in a musician's life, very valuable colleagues don't make it all the way, and leave us with a deep sorrow upon their departure. That was the case October 30, 2013 when we received the sad news of our dearest saxophonist and flutist Frank Wess's passing. He was ninety-two and a true pioneer of the flute in jazz. Frank was a very funny guy that told us incredible anecdotes of the days when he played with Ellington, Gillespie, and other famous ones.

Frank was once part of an excellent quartet that always played wearing tuxedos as a touch of elegance and class. The bassist in this quartet was something out of the ordinary as a soloist, and a solid accompanist. It was hard for Wess and the rest of the quartet to understand how such a formidable instrumentalist drank like such a fish. Sometimes he couldn't even walk straight or articulate words, but in a concert he didn't miss a note. He played it all—harmony, rhythm, melody, and solos with unbelievable perfection—when everyone knew he was completely drunk.

One night the bass player drank even more than usual and left the theater, practically lurching on his hands and knees in an unknown direction. Everyone was worried, since the next morning they were flying to New York, so they retired early, praying that their friend would make it on time. His room was next door to Frank Wess's room, who told me that when he left for the airport at five in the morning, he found the bassist still in his tuxedo and bowtie, lying on the floor next to his bass, head resting on his left arm and his room key in his hand.

The older guys always have funny anecdotes to share, like when Carlos "Patato" Valdés told me something interesting about Arsenio Rodríguez. "The Marvelous Blind Man" was the nickname given to the tres player native to Güira de Macurijes in the Matanzas Province. He was an extraordinary artist, very original and innovative, and had a great many admirers and followers among musicians who had worked with him, both in his native Cuba and later in the United States where he moved during the late 1940s.

But Patato tells me that sometimes Arsenio would get slippery with the musicians' money. One time, during the height of his popularity on the New York dance scene, at the end of a gig in front of a full house, the musicians approached Arsenio to collect the agreed-upon money.

Then the blind musician just shrugged his shoulders, arguing, "Well, gentlemen, you've seen for yourselves the way this gig turned out, haven't you?"

Patato retorted, "Coño, of course I saw it, but it looks like the only one who didn't see it was you."

The famous soprano Martina Arroyo is a unique and exquisite character whose presence is always a reason to celebrate for those of us who have enjoyed the privilege of her company. Daughter of a Puerto Rican immigrant and a black mother from South Carolina, Martina grew up in Harlem and was exposed to a diverse array of artistic and cultural manifestations since her infancy; her father earned a good living as a mechanical engineer on ships in Brooklyn, so the family was able to visit museums and expositions and see concerts, theater, and opera frequently.

It was these activities and her subsequent studies in literature and singing lessons that helped her develop a sensitivity toward the arts in the young daughter of Demetrio Arroyo and Lucille Washington. In time, the future grand diva of opera houses such as Covent Garden, Scala de Milan, the National Opera in París, the Colón Theater in Buenos Aires, Deutsche Oper Berlin, the San Francisco Opera, and New York's Metropolitan Opera House became part of the first generation of successful singers to break through the barrier of racial prejudice in the exclusive world of the opera.

During her long and triumphant career, Martina interpreted the most famous roles in the repertory, among them "The

Valkyrie," from the Wagnerian tetralogy "Ring of the Nibelung." Apparently, the diva's mother would break out in laughter at the site of her daughter, with black eyes and velvet skin as dark as the night, taking the stage and shouting over the orchestra, wearing that Nordic blonde wig and braids as required for the Broom-Hilda character. Our mutual friend, Puerto Rican soprano Thelma Ithier, who regularly attended functions at the Met, tells me that everybody, including Martina, knew when her mother was in the house because Lucille Washington Arroyo's laughter echoed throughout the chamber.

Martina Arroyo inherited from her mother a sense of humor and a joy for life that are contagious. Her husband, French-born Michel Maurel, is the person who most enjoys the things she says. Her intense, penetrating eyes reflect intelligence, sincerity, and tenderness. One time she made me laugh so much with her antics that I said to her, "You ought to be a comedian, Martina."

"What do you mean 'ought to be'?" she replied. "I *am* a comedian! It's just that I'm trapped in this opera thing, can't you see?"

I met her personally at a "Jazz Masters" event in New York, backstage in the Grand Ballroom of the Marriot Marquis hotel in Times Square. A row of chairs had been placed with our names on each so that we would be seated in the order in which we'd be called to the stage. Present that day, among others were Dave Brubeck, Nancy Wilson, the Heath brothers Percy and Jimmy, George Benson, Freddie Hubbard, Buddy DeFranco, and David Baker, whose seat was next to mine.

Imagine my surprise upon arriving at my seat, when I find, in Professor Baker's place, an illustrious lyrical personality having little or nothing to do with the jazz world—the one and only Martina Arroyo. I sat down, greeted the people around me, turned to her, and asked, "Excuse me, madam, but aren't you Martina Arroyo?"

"And what do you think," the diva replied, her expressive eyes open wide. "That I'm David Baker?"

The laughter of those nearby coincided with the arrival of the real David Baker, who knew from the laughs that Martina had been up to her antics again. It turns out they taught together in college and had been friends for many years. It was David who invited her to the event that evening. Later on, by coincidence, she was seated at the same table as my wife. Brenda even took a vocal master class with her, and the friendship between our family and the "Valkiria of Ebony" has been consolidated.

Cláudio Roditi worked for a long time in my quintet, back in the mid-'80s with Lincoln Goines, Portinho, and Michel Camilo. That was a beautiful time for me, exploring Brazilian music. Although he was Dominican, Michel knew the style well. Lincoln had worked extensively with Raul de Souza, Leny Andrade, and other artists who cultivated the genre. Cláudio, from whom we learned much, had achieved the perfect combination between bebop and the music of his native land.

In those days, we played a club at Ninety-Sixth Street and Columbus, Mikel's, whose owner Pat Mikel was a very good-looking middle-aged blonde. At one of those jams, Cláudio couldn't make it, due to an engagement in Europe, so he recommended the formidable trombonist Conrad Herwig, who quickly demonstrated his ability to read and perfectly transpose the parts written for Cláudio's trumpet.

Conrad always had an inclination towards Latin American music. Years later he would go on to collaborate with Latin giants like Eddie Palmieri and Mario Bauzá, as well as on the "Latin Sides" of jazz artists such as Miles Davis, John Coltrane, and Wayne Shorter, receiving both nominations and Grammys for some of those recordings.

The small stage at Mikel's was in front of the bar, next to a stairwell door that led to the dressing rooms and restrooms located in the basement. During that first set with Conrad filling in for Cláudio, I remember we were playing a bossa nova and Michel was taking his piano solo when a tall woman with short hair, glasses, skin-tight jeans, and a jumbo-sized ass got up from the bar, walked by the musicians, and disappeared through the stairwell door. I was literally hypnotized as I watched that thing pass, and when I couldn't see it anymore, I said to Conrad, who spoke a little Spanish, "Wow! Did you see the ass on her?"

"Thank you," he said.

I was perplexed and clarified: "What do you mean, 'thank you'? I was talking about *her* ass."

"She's my wife," he replied from his six-foot five-inch height.

And that was the end of that conversation. I didn't know what to say or where to hide and would've wanted the earth to open up and swallow me whole at that moment, but, like Woody Allen says, comedy is tragedy plus time. Now we laugh together about the incident.

According to a survey conducted years ago, there were many instances of depression among symphony musicians. However, having performed that type of work for some time, I can tell you first-hand that it's a lot of fun and that on occasion just to be in the presence of the grand orchestra is enough for the unexpected to occur.

Many years ago, during a snowstorm at an airport, I had the good fortune of meeting the members of The Turtle Island Quartet, a marvelous group I had admired for many years through their many recordings. We clicked almost immediately; I agreed to send them a copy of my *Wapango*, which they "Turtleized" in their unique style. Then later, by way of the American Chamber Music Society, I had a major work commissioned especially for them, which I entitled "La Jicotea," after the little green turtle that lives in rivers and lagoons throughout the Caribbean.

One of the members of the group was the extraordinary viola player Danny Seidenberg, a true master of his instrument. He's what I call a "barking cat," which is as close as you'll come to a viola player with swing (there aren't many). Danny is a dark-humored and mysterious cat. He's kind of grumpy, says the funniest things when he tries to talk seriously, and frequently finds himself in crazier situations than you could imagine.

On this particular day he arrived very early to a rehearsal at Carnegie Hall with New York's Philharmonic and sat down in the viola row to study some papers he found on the stand… But let Danny be the one to tell it in his own words:

I guess this story is emblematic of the freelance musician experience in New York, running from job to job and rehearsal to rehearsal every day for dozens of different groups and venues; it's so easy to make a mistake. It also reflects the New York City Danny of the 1980s—young, a bit wild, a little spaced out, long-haired, and kind of counter culture-ish.

It was a normal workday (I seem to remember it being April 1987), and I had a full schedule ahead—an orchestra rehearsal at Carnegie Hall, a recording session in the afternoon, and a concert in the evening. I took the E train in from Queens wearing my concert clothes, as there would be no time to go home before the performance. How ridiculous, walking around in a tailcoat tuxedo all day, but that's what I often did. I had my New York Post rolled up under my arm and my viola slung from my shoulder. I grabbed my regular coffee in the blue and white cup from a deli on Seventh Avenue and proceeded to Carnegie.

In through the stage door and onto the stage at 9:50 for what I believed was going to be a ten a.m. rehearsal of the American Composers Orchestra. There was no security in those days. I had made my way over to the viola section, sat down in my chair, unpacked, and started to tune, when I felt quizzical stares coming my way. I realized that I didn't recognize anyone and people were speaking German. Then I remembered the program had some contemporary German composers, and I thought that explained it, but I became uneasy because eyes were all still turning toward me.

I reached for my trusty datebook to confirm the service and—uh oh! My rehearsal was not at Carnegie but at Avery Fisher Hall in Lincoln Center. I looked at the stand in front of me; the folder said Vienna Philharmonic. The warm-up sounds stopped, and there was a murmur of conversation and finger-pointing.

Red-faced and embarrassed, I packed up and ran off the stage. As I hurried through the wings I ran straight into someone headed toward the stage. It was Leonard Bernstein, on his way in to start the rehearsal.

He stopped and beamed at me, "Well… Hello!"

"Excuse me, Maestro," I muttered.

Out into the street, grabbed a cab and made my way up to Lincoln Center. The rehearsal was in progress… I was late. I went to the contractor who was playing the French horn, apologized, explained what had happened, and asked him not to tell anyone what I had done. He laughed and laughed. By the time the break came people were looking at me and giggling. Some came up to me and spoke German. It went on for years like that; even musicians whom I had never met knew the story. I think everyone who had this singular New York experience related to it.

Later, another incident occurred in a ballet pit, when an entire bag of confetti was dropped by a dancer on my head during a Nutcracker performance. Another time a contra bassoon player barfed on my shoe during Mahler's "Resurrection" Symphony. There were countless incidents like that; I seemed to attract them.

The Elephant and his Three Tigers

I swore never to be silent whenever and wherever human beings endure suffering and humiliation.... Neutrality helps the oppressor, never the victim. Silence encourages the tormentor, never the tormented.
—Elie Wiesel

I spent a great deal of my youth at Tropicana, Yeyito, where "A Paradise Under the Stars" was the advertising slogan. Have you ever been there? Well, at the "most beautiful nightclub in the world," there were dancers, jugglers, musicians, and famous singers, but you would also be sure to find several entertainment critics, script writers, playwrights, interviewers, and journalists in any and all of the three huge halls—every specimen of the Cuban Night's diverse gamut.

Among the Tropicana musicians was Rubén Romeu, who played baritone saxophone and sometimes the violin in his brother Armando's orchestra. Between shows, you could find him in a corner under a palm tree or at a distant table at the employee coffee shop, writing the next chapter of *Divorciadas* or any other successful radio serial for the many stations he wrote for during the '40s and '50s.

"Listen, Rubén," people following the adventures of his radio characters would tell him. "Yesterday you threw your protagonist off a cliff and there are ten more chapters to go... What will you do next?"

Inevitably the next day, something happened to save the victim; either a parachute came out unexpectedly from the hero's backpack or the guy was rescued by a phoenix in the midst of the dramatic fall. Then that evening Rubén arrived triumphant at Tropicana's coffee shop and was received with bells and whistles as if he himself was the hero of his own story.

Around that time I was nine or ten, and my father bought me my first literary masterpiece, *Sandokán the Tiger of Malaysia* at La Moderna Poesía, a beautiful bookstore on Obispo Street. Emilio Salgari's novel fascinated me, and soon after I was reading *The Black Corsair*, *The Tigers of Mompracem*, *The Ghost Ship*, and *The King of the Sea*, written mostly by the writer from Verona. In those days there was no Internet, so the fact that Emilio Salgari had never traveled further than the Adriatic Sea remained a legend. All those fantasy oceans and hallucinatory adventures had come completely from the Italian writer's imagination, which made them even more fascinating. Shortly after that came the stories of Verne, Daudet, Zweig, José Eustasio Rivera, Flaubert, and Salvador de Madariaga. I read whatever book I found on the white wooden bookshelf my father kept in the hallway, next to a vertical piano. Quickly, my devotion to those people that could, from the touch of a pen, create, describe, and narrate events that may or may not have happened grew more and more. Over time, I've had the privilege of making friends with my literary and journalistic idols, and I've declared my love to many of them. Sooner or later they became victims of my persistent persecution.

I wrote Zoé Valdés from a Caribbean island, having just read her *Nada cotidiana* (Everyday Nothingness) on my flight from New York. I wrote on the postcard, "If you like, I'll leave complimentary tickets to my Paris New Morning concert next month," and she accepted.

I got to Carlos Alberto Montaner through my old friends Normita and Marcos Miranda, a radio and TV writing couple that worked with Carlos Alberto in Madrid. I went to the editorial office of the weekly *The Village Voice* in Manhattan looking for Nat Hentoff to give him a beautiful *guayabera* and to thank him for his huge contribution in documenting music and jazz musicians, as well as for his noble and energetic defense of human rights in Cuba and around the world.

Writer Eliseo Alberto, or "Lichy" as we affectionately called the very talented son of Eliseo Diego, was an extraordinary guy. He was fast and sharp. Once he came to New York for a presentation of his novel *Caracol Beach*. Once the moderator introduced him and gave him the microphone, Lichy took it and stared at it for a few seconds.

"Never give a microphone to a Cuban so easily," he said. "He might talk non-stop for fifty years or more."

Everyone laughed out loud. Lichy was that spontaneous. His premature death due to cancer (although he was often warned about nicotine), filled us all with despair. Constante "Rapi" Diego, his younger brother had a similar ending from the same cause. It is proven that no one learns from the advice of others.

The particular case of my friendship with Guillermo Cabrera Infante is very special, because he's one of the Cuban writers most associated with the musical world, jazz, and, of course, Cuban nightlife.

It all began one afternoon at the end of the '60s at the Antillas Bar of the Hotel Habana Libre (old Hilton). The bar is located at the entrance of the Salón Caribe, where the show goes on every night. As you probably remember, musicians and "night people" used to call it "Las Cañitas," because it is surrounded by bamboo.

Since it was still early, the bar was deserted. I was alone on one of the wicker stools drinking a Cuba libre. There were only a couple of Canadian tourists sipping their mojitos slowly and ceremoniously at the small tables, when my friend Nicolás Reinoso walked in hastily. Without even saying hello, taking advantage that the barman was far from us catering to the tourists, Nicolás looked around, took a book from his pocket, and passed it to me.

"Take a discreet glance at this book," he said. "If you're interested, take it home, but return it as soon as you read it. It belongs to a friend from the Spanish embassy."

The book was *Tres tristes tigres* by Guillermo Cabrera Infante, who, like many other persona-non-grata authors unwelcomed by the cultural authorities of the island, was forbidden. You could only acquire it through someone who brought it from the outside, said El Negro, although it was us who were on the outside of everything.

Chino Infante's emblematic novel became a true symbol to young people like me who tried uselessly to reconstruct and build over the ruins of Havana, the hallucinatory environment that the writer from Gibara described so masterfully in those pages. Since that time, the tribulations of Bustrofedón, Arsenio Cué, the Star, and the rest of Infante's characters remained forever encrusted in my mind.

That is, until November 1981, when Dizzy Gillespie hired me for a European tour that included a couple of nights at the famous Ronnie Scott's Jazz Club in London. I knew of cinematographer Jorge Ulla's relationship with the almost mythological G. Cain, Cabrera Infante's pseudonym when he wrote for *Carteles* magazine. It was Ulla who gave me his telephone number in the city of Sherlock Holmes, where he lived.

"Hello… Miriam, it's me, Paquito, inviting you to Dizzy's show at Soho's Ronnie Scott's."

I left the names of Mr. and Mrs. Cabrera Infante on the guest list that evening. At the end of the show, the couple came backstage to meet Dizzy Gillespie, a legendary character for Cabrera Infante, who was always a modern jazz lover.

"We almost didn't get in!" said his charming wife Miriam.

"It was sold out," Guillermo added. "And they listed our names as Mr. and Mrs. Elefante!"

This made Dizzy laugh. He never learned the writer's name and always called him Señor Elefante. Two days later, an extensive and beautiful article from Cabrera Infante about our presentation in the club was published in an important London newspaper.

My admired fellow countryman would later write several notes for the back covers of my records and the prologue for the Spanish edition of my first book, *My Sax Life*. In the form of revenge, as he used to say, I then wrote a piece for three basses called "Tres Tristes Tigres." One of the basses was

Cachao, and it was recorded on my album *40 Years of Cuban Jam Session*, a fun Miami project in which our common friend Andy García played the bongo.

The last time I saw Cabrera alive was at the end of a concert with Yo-Yo Ma in London. His health was already in decline, and his demeanor was fragile and painful. He hugged me, and while he did, the image of that November 1981 evening at Ronnie Scott's came to mind. It had marked the beginning of a beautiful and lasting friendship, one that flourished from my deep admiration and originated at the bar of the magical city the author of *Vista del amanecer en el trópico* (*A View of Dawn in the Tropics*) so passionately loved and to which he sang praises through time and space like no one else did, "with a tiger's voice and an elephant's memory," until the very day of his death.

Speaking of writers and writings, Yeyito, there's a place that has a lot to do with magic realism that is so much talked about in Latin American literature. I'm talking about Veracruz, whose nights' magic reality would make Kafka's stories and Fellini's movies turn pale. I heard about Veracruz in 1953 when my dad came back fascinated by a tour of México with the infantry band. Fifty-some years later I made it to beautiful Veracruz, after playing a couple of concerts with the Xalapa Symphony Orchestra under the baton of the young and talented director Carlos Miguel Prieto. It is true that it's beautiful and warm, although what they say about it resembling Havana is as doubtful as what Lorca says about Havana being "Cádiz with more *negritos*." They have tried to compare the Cuban capital to many cities, but it takes a bit more than negritos and one or two *danzonera* playing on the street to complete the hallucinatory formula of the "City of Columns." Like that one, there's none other in the whole world. Cádiz is Cádiz, mysterious as the elf in the flamenco piano of its illustrious son Chano Domínguez. Port Veracruz is airy, sunny, joyful, and definitely charming.

One of the first literary works my old man recommended and I read several times was Salvador de Madariaga's *Hernán Cortés y la Conquista de la Nueva España* (Hernan Cortés and the Conquest of New Spain). It was an apotheosis, a passionate book that placed in my infantile mind the vision of one day visiting the mouth of the river where the ships of the navigator from Extremadura entered, touching the ancestral Ceiba tree where they tied the ship, which for some reason is now on firm land (in Latin America even the high tide is temperamental).

My pianist, Alon Yavnai, and his Spanish-Venezuelan-Australian-Iranian wife Julie Criniére, who is an excellent photographer, stayed with us for the Veracruz adventure. Together we visited the stone house that Cortés built in the outskirts of the city. Malinche, the mythical native that bewitched him with her charms, mother of his *mestizo* children, lived there. She learned the language of his soldiers, guided him, served as his interpreter, and helped him betray the great Moctezuma.

Julie Creniére took the prettiest images of the home's ruins and of the small chapel in town. The church was kept fairly well, but the historic mansion is completely abandoned by the Mexican authorities. The greatest tourist guides are the neighborhood's children; they take the visitors through the debris, where anyone (even me) can take home one of the several centuries-old stones brought from the Old World in the sixteenth century. Climbing plants and trees have remained for centuries wrapped around walls that would have fallen apart if it weren't for them. Next to the ruins was a broken-down and darkened shack, and in its patio there was a clothesline with recently-washed clothes. In the center, over a wooden stake, was a rusty fifty-five-gallon container cut in half. Something was boiling in it, filling the environment with a grayish vapor. Hens, ducks, and pigs ran around the mud, and ants walked with discipline hauling their loads between emerging roots that look like tentacles on the floor. A huge blackish-green chameleon watched upside down from his tower over a willowy tree. Mariachi trumpets jumped out from the torn speaker of a portable radio, contrasting with the hoarse sounds of the big Mexican guitar known as the *guitarrón*. On the other side of the rustic wire netting a horde of filthy, colorful, street dogs camped out. This is where history converges with the historic Latin American poverty, hierarchy with indigence. This is also where one can appreciate (or despise) the indolent irresponsibility of certain politicians regarding the preservation of national relics. The scene reminded me of the time in Italy, when we found an old toilet in the ruins of the Roman Forum. Spaniards would say that it could happen anywhere, but I should say they do preserve their national relics.

The danzón is kept much more alive in Mexico than in Cuba, its birthplace. They say it's because during the second half of the twentieth century, its creator, Matanzas-born cornet player Miguel Faílde and his popular orchestra came every year to play in the famous festivities of the Veracruz Fair. The danzón is so deeply rooted in the heart of Mexicans that even

American composer Aaron Copland, in addition to his "Danzón Cubano," wrote another symphonic danzón and called it "Salón México," which, in my opinion, is a lot better than the first one.

El Zócalo, where a danzonera orchestra plays in between a museum's column, is in the heart of Veracruz. Dancers come in every Wednesday afternoon to dance only danzones. The orchestra has a typical structure similar to Faílde 's: two clarinets, a cornet, trombone, *güiro*, and two *timbalones*. In the one I saw that afternoon, they had added two saxophones to the original format. Elegantly dressed dancers either in guayaberas or linen suits and their mates in linen dresses and high heels wait graciously with their fans while the orchestra plays the *paseo* before they begin dancing to the tune. Then back to the paseo for a short rest period, and then to enjoy the *montuno*!

All of a sudden, between the shadows of the gateways, as if running away from a García Márquez story, the fragile figure of a tiny seventy-something woman appeared. She walked so lightly that it seemed she didn't even touch the floor with her white canvas slippers. She wore white satin stockings that fell softly on her thin ballerina ankles. She wore a pink lace dress with silk ribbons. Her braids were carefully interwoven on her doll-like head, where a tiara with her name on it spread rays of light. Charito, the Queen of Danzón had arrived with her flowered fan, supported by the arm of her escort, a tall corpulent man of coppery skin and strong but pleasant features. His whitest guayabera matched his carefully shined impeccable two-tone shoes. A wide brim Jipi-Japa hat worn slightly to the side on his gray hair seemed to greet everyone as the wind whipped. Charito and her beau organized the couples as if tropicalizing the minuet. It was a pleasure to see these dance aficionados looking like a disciplined classical ballet company.

I had my cell phone on me, and miraculously on the first try I communicated with my friend Félix Durán. He happened to be home in the town of Minas, in the outskirts of Havana. When I told him what I was watching and he listened to the danzonera playing "Las Alturas de Simpson" (they say "Simpson's Heights" was the first danzón in history), I could feel the emotion in my friend's voice on the other side.

"People here don't even remember that," he said sadly.

I was excited, too, like I was during my first trip to Panama, when pianist Danilo Pérez's father took me to the home of a collector of Cuban music and memorabilia. There, I was unfazed by the usual poster of Che Guevara, his eyes lost in the horizon, or by the little *pioneritos* with red bandanas, militia men armed to their teeth, or junky old American cars parked on the streets of a Havana devastated by socialist "progress." Instead, I was amazed that on the walls of his music room hung a picture of Celia Cruz, next to one of Benny Moré, with his brimmed hat and cane, dancing in front of his "Tribe," as he called his giant band. On the extreme left of the saxophone lineup I recognized Virgilio "El Jamaiquino" with his big African monarch's face, playing his baritone, wearing his beige gabardine uniform.

On the conga drum in the corner of the room, there was a patch where you could see white and maroon shoes.

"Those are my Cuban shoes for dancing *el son*," said our Panamanian host.

I felt proud to see the passion, love, and joy my country's artists had spread all over the world. A wandering people's only source of happiness is its unnerving, sweet, and sensual music.

The afternoon began to fade in the city, letting the yellow streetlights shine. Stars sparkled in the sky, and a full moon lit the Veracruz night. The glowing Zócalo floor ceramics seemed to have life of their own with the reflection of thousands of little light bulbs that embraced the tree trunks and the surrounding palm trees. The danzoneros picked up their belongings, for Jarocho harps, marimbas, mariachi musicians, and all sorts of street artists and characters took over the night. A street vendor that obviously made many that afternoon had filled the space with huge helium inflatable pencils. The colorful metallic balloons flew in slow motion back and forth in the park. Dogs barked frantically and ran as if watching the air. Each child had his own flying pencil, and the ones who didn't had sharp nails to pop them. The crying would begin inevitably after each blowout. Or the fight between the pencil owner and the pencil popper. Marx would have said, "Oh, the eternal class struggle!" while spreading his black caviar on toast.

A bearded, dark-skinned, tattered crazy man passed by waving a small Cuban flag, while he proclaimed his merchandise for sale: "Candy, peanuts, Caranga water, Orisa oil, Turkish soap, raisins, pears, grapes, sons, red apples (and the other kind), hot tamales, earrings, rings, thimbles, needles, fine scissors, grinding stones, thread, all kinds of ribbons, and colorful straps!" I remember the whole inventory, because while he shouted, he gave out flyers with a list of the strange products he wasn't even carrying with him.

"Cubans are odd, mister…" said the little old man limping in his worn-out *guaraches*. He carried a large, dented bass-tuba around his body. His teeny eyes shone under the straw hat pulled over his ears. He was dressed all in white, with a big cotton camisole and pants above his ankles, as if playing a member of General Pancho Villa's rebel troops in a film. The old man blew on his instrument with such staggering power that the street vendor jumped high, like a scared rabbit.

The zany man turned around waving his fist high, damning the little old man that scared him. Then he rushed through the multitude divulging his merchandise out loud: "Candies, peanut bags, specialty waters and oil extracts, Turkish soaps, raisins, pears, grapes, sons, red and not-so-red apples, hot-and not-so-hot tamales, earrings, rings, thimbles, needles, fine scissors, sharpening stones, all kinds of thread and multicolor ribbons…" until he (and his echo) disappeared in the crowd.

"Cubans are odd? Is he asking or telling me?" my wife asked.

All of a sudden, a very thin man in a pirate costume showed up. He had high boots and balloon sleeves and was spitting out large balls of fire. He had a sword on his snakeskin belt, also a short musket and a long black whip he cracked every once in a while, mainly to get attention. A red scarf tied on his head, a golden ring on one ear, and a black patch that covered one of his eyes made him look quite ferocious. After the fire act, he swallowed the sword to the hilt. "Ooooohhhhhh!" Exclaimed an exalted multitude, following his every move. To end his performance, the filibuster fired his musket in the air, leaving the smell of gunpowder and a dark cloud in the environment.

On the other side of the park, we could hear the monot-onous sharp and repetitive sound of a wooden flute. We got closer to the observing bystanders' circle and we saw four native men doing an incredible balancing act. While three of them tied by their ankles intertwined their strings around themselves, the fourth one played his tiny wind instrument from a very high pole, dancing on a small platform atop what looked like the mast of a ship.

They were Papantla Flyers, part of a tradition that goes back to pre-Columbian days. I remembered something funny my friend Mexican sculptor Carlos Aguilar y Linares told me once. The news once reported that Interpol surrounded an airplane with thieves and their loot escaping from Mexico and stopped it in the air. The newscaster, realizing the absurdity of the information he was given, quickly added, "So we suspect the agents were probably trained by the Flyers of Papantla."

Awnings and huge umbrellas of different designs both bore logos of the most diverse products and served as partitions between the many restaurants next to the plaza. The smell of the street vendors' goods and the fried food outdoors made us hungry. Brenda came up with the idea of dining in one of those *típico* restaurants. We soon found out that the option of street vendor foods would have been more practical and relaxed.

"Gooooooool!" shouted the football fans following the game at the inside bar.

Our waiter, a big fifty-something Mexican of tanned complexion, jet-black hair, and such a happy face that he smiled from ear to ear, explained: "Mexico is winning and that was the decisive goal."

"Why are you laughing so heartily, *manito*?" I asked the server.

He answered in that fun, spicy way some Mexicans have when expressing themselves: "Why am I laughing, boss? For the tears the friggin' Italians must be shedding after that goal we managed to sneak in. Did you see that, boss?"

As soon as the smiling waiter brought us the menus and the beers we had ordered, a lady with braids, a long multicolored skirt, and a white blouse with floral decorations around the neck appeared. Hanging from her waist was a board with the most unusual combination of fans, peanuts, necklaces, cheeses, sweets, and salads. Brenda already had a fan she always carried with her, Julie didn't want anything, and we couldn't think of a reason to buy peanuts, cheese, or salads sitting at a restaurant, so we politely bid the lady farewell.

A little boy who looked like a direct descendant of Moctezuma sang to us: "Guantanamera, guajira Guantanamera." He had a little red gourd that he played by scratching it with a wooden stick. I threw a coin in the hole of the gourd. But not even three minutes had gone by when: "Guantanamera, guajira Guantanamera." It was the boy's little sister, singing the same song but accompanying herself with a little blue gourd instead (orchestral colors, as Rimsky Korsakov would have pointed out).

A bit later, a lonesome man in a *charro* costume approached us playing a small black contrabass with three white strings mounted on a rubber wheel. He had a huge hat and a silver-plated revolver on his belt. He said good evening and placed four small black folders with gold letters that read "Musical Menu" on the table. When you opened them, you could see dozens of song titles classified by genre, from *guarachas*,

Peruvian waltzes, and Agustin Lara's *boleros* to *corridos*, fox-trots, and huapangos.

"No thanks," said Alón, returning the four folders to the man.

He refused to give up and sang an unending potpourri of Cuban songs with his potent, out-of tune tenor voice, accompanied by his pigmy bass. I felt sorry for the guy and reached across to give him a coin.

When I tried to bring my hand back, a dark hand with the reddest nails and covered with fancy rings grabbed mine, turning it palm up. It was a fat gipsy of indefinite age, just like the ones you might see on the streets of Seville, Budapest, or Punta del Este.

"Hmmm! You're going to have much success in your life, my love, but a selfish, marvelous, and unscrupulous woman will try to come between you," pronounced the gypsy, her eyes flashing as she pointed at Julie, assuming she was my wife. Her brusque motion made the bracelets and chains that covered her thick trembling hands give off a chiming sound. We laughed loudly at the woman's confusion, and she in turn, smelling foot-in-mouth, left abruptly without saying goodbye and got lost in the crowd.

From that group of gypsies emerged the unexpected figure of a youth, normal height, with short black hair, some locks sprinkled with gold and bright blue. He wore a silver shirt, pointed shoes the same color, bright orange pants, and purple rim glasses, which made him look like an explorer from another planet. He carried the case of some string instrument in his hand and was saying goodbye to the gypsies as if he were another member of the tribe, or at least a life-long friend. It was the ineffable Inti Bullón, the son of a Peruvian cellist with the Xalapa Orchestra.

A talented musician, Inti is also quite a character. As charismatic as he is enigmatic, the young musician plays (and very well) a chartreuse-colored viola, in the same orchestra as his dad, and with various chamber music groups. Everything about him is remarkable, indicating to a high sense of individualism and innate sense of originality. Let's just say you don't run into people like him every day.

"Hey, Inti, where you rushing off to? Have a little shot of tequila with us," I told him.

But the likeable musician, always courteous and well-mannered, came over to our table and declined our invitation. In that peculiar voice of his, like Yogi the Bear from the Huckleberry Hound cartoons, he told us, "They are waiting for me—first the leuthier who repairs my instrument and then a hair stylist friend of mine."

"At this hour?" I was surprised.

"Yes, the thing is, tomorrow I have to rehearse with a very conservative conductor who doesn't like the color of my viola or my hair, and they're going to do me the favor of—oh well, see what strange things happen to me? Anyway, *ciao*."

Inti Bullón said goodbye with his sweet smile of a gentle Martian, when all of sudden, a deafening drumroll made us jump out of our seats. When we looked up we saw a short, skinny, boney individual that looked like a jockey. He wore a suit similar to Superman's but with an *R* on the chest. A light blue brief contrasted with his yellow leotard. A red cape covered his shoulders. He had tied a fluorescent rope from one tree to the other, and when the drumroll stopped he left the drumsticks on the drum, dropped his cape, and announced himself as "Raymond the Incredible." He immediately jumped on top of the tightrope and started to do circus juggling acts; he pulled out the fringed umbrellas, jumped rope, put a skate on his head, and glided upside down from end to end on the tightrope. When he finished, he came down to play another drumroll. Afterwards he blindfolded himself and grabbed a long stick he had next to a silver-plated monocycle waiting for its turn next to a tree. Again he jumped on the scaffold and felt his way slowly and dramatically crossing the rope from one side to the other. While this happened, an eight- or ten-year-old barefoot child wearing canvas pants that once were white ran desperately to the unicycle. He got on it with surprising dexterity and, like a lightening bolt, disappeared down the dark street at full speed. Surprised, Alon, Julie, Brenda, and I, next to some Americans at the next table, started to applaud frantically, thinking it was part of Incredible Raymond's act.

"The *Huachinango* strikes again!" a little voice behind us said firmly. It was Charito, the Queen of Danzón, with a box of chocolate sneakers for sale in her hands.

"Huachinango?" we all asked at the same time.

The ancient dancer explained: "The danzones orchestra you saw this afternoon in the courtyard used to play outside until the Huachinango, that demon who stole Raymond's unicycle, climbed to the roof of the museum and urinated into the bell of Lupe's tuba, the blind lady who played at the danzonera."

The gringas at the next table sighed in amazement, and I had to hold my laughter, remembering my mischievous childhood.

"Sealed the misdemeanor in gold, wetting the whole orchestra," the little old lady added, lifting her index finger.

We all looked in the direction that the fearsome Huachinango had fled, pursued by Raymond the Incredible, but the only thing we were able to spot among the shadows was the far, far away silhouette of Inti carrying his controversial green viola's case.

It had been a long, hard journey, and the exhaustion of the busy day crept up on us. Now the smells of the gunpowder and alcohol from the pirate pervaded the humid air and mixed with the sweaty and exciting fragrance of the flashy ladies of the twilight. We walked back down the old cobblestone Veracruz streets, surrounded by the warmth of its people, the cries of the street hawkers, the sounds of the street musicians, and the unreal and fascinating light of its starry nights.

A soft breeze was blowing in from the port. As we strolled by the seawall, we saw in the distance the imposingly enormous statue of Venustiano Carranza by the lighthouse that also bears his name. As soon as I got back to the hotel I fell into a deep sleep and dreamt I was playing danzones in the gardens of the mansion of Hernán Cortés. The dream was so real that I could even smell the delicate fragrance of the aleli flowers and saw the Conquistador dancing cheek-to-cheek with La Malinche to the beat of an orchestra made up of my friend Alón on harpsichord, the charro on bass, the flutist from the Flyers of Papantla, and the twins on gourds. The old man of the helicon backed up the black street hawker, and with them, Inti Bullón, with his multi-colored hair and his musical Martian glasses, carried the melody with his inseparable green viola. Sheer magic realism!

Generoso Jiménez died a few years ago in Miami, and I never had the opportunity to ask him about the legitimacy of the story my father had told me. He was a good friend from his youth, many years back. If it is true, then the eminent musician, born in the town of Cruces, belonged to the same club of that Spaniard that is known to have said, "Since the bidet was invented, women have lost their flavor."

The Hard One

Tom is a Boy, Mary is a Girl.
—Dr. Leonardo Sorzano Jorrín

I was a kid in Havana when I had my first encounter with what Cuban percussionist Daniel Ponce used to call "The Ultimate Challenge" (i.e. the English language). My dad showed up at home one day with a Benny Goodman LP recorded live at some place called "Carnegie Hall." Surprised, I asked, "What do you mean, *carne y frijol*?" I couldn't see any possible connection between the dish my mother cooked all the time and that exciting music played by the Jewish clarinetist and his orchestra.

About twenty-five years after my father practically choked in laughter from my unintentional joke, when I was on tour with my band Irakere, I was having breakfast in a coffee shop on Broadway. Come to think of it, it was actually very near Carnegie Hall ("carne y frijol"). While we were waiting for our food, I heard one of the musicians from the band trying to use English to explain to a CBS executive that he wasn't feeling well. He said that he had eaten too much the night before and woke up with "*estrenyimyent.*"

Wagging his head from side to side, like a dog who doesn't understand what you're trying to teach him, the American tried to pronounce this strange word: "Estrenyimyent?"

The musician was trying to say that he was having trouble voiding his bowels, in other words that he was suffering from "*estreñimiento*" or constipation. As I recall, the person who produced that strange Hispanicism from out of left field got seriously ticked off when the saxophonist Carlos Averhoff, who was also at our table, almost fell off his seat laughing. Well, all I can say is that the Spanglish that has become a part of our everyday speech is one thing, but utter nonsense is something else altogether, and it can trigger some pretty hysterical situations.

When I had finally moved to New York City, toward the end of 1980, one of my first jobs was substituting for José Fajardo, the famous Cuban flute player. He was so popular that he sometimes had as many as two or three orchestras playing at once in different parts of the city.

In those days I still lived with my mother in the Overlook Terrace building in West New York, New Jersey, and since Fajardo lived in the same building, he gave me a ride in his enormous station wagon one freezing Sunday to La Bilbaína restaurant on Twenty-Third Street in Manhattan. The plan was that I would take his place in the band while he went on to Brooklyn, where he had another gig. His son Armandito was already playing the timbal from time to time with Fajardo and His Stars, so he came along with us. Having been born in the United States, Armandito was perfectly bilingual and would often help his monolingual dad make himself understood.

The afternoon was clear, peaceful, and bright, and a light but chilling breeze blew over from the Hudson River, mixing with the delicious smell of Cuban cooking that emanated from Overlook Terrace. When we got out to the parking lot, people who recognized the legendary Fajardo greeted him with affection and enthusiasm. As soon as he started the engine the radio began blasting the lively notes of "Sayonara, Sayonara, I'm Off to Japan," one of the hits that Fajardo, a country boy from Pinar del Río, had at the end of the '50s. The radio was tuned to our neighbor Polito Vega's weekly program. Polito was a star DJ in the city.

As José, Armandito, and I started making our way up Boulevard East toward the Lincoln Tunnel, the impressive profile of the City of Skyscrapers appeared to move along the horizon as if it were alive. A group of children was placing floral offerings next to the bust of Cuban patriot José Martí on its marble pedestal in the park along the eastern sidewalk of the street.

I told the Fajardos, "They say one time in a class he was teaching, Martí pronounced Shakespeare's name as if it were in Spanish: *Chah-Keh-SPEER-eh.* When one of the students corrected him, Martí continued the rest of the lesson in perfect English."

Fajardo replied with his usual grin, "Well, *hermano,* good thing I wasn't in that class, because it would've all been Greek to me, *sabes?*"

On the way to La Bilbaína, we stopped at a gas station to fill up the enormous station wagon's gluttonous tank. "*Filirópalo, primo!*" the elder Fajardo called out in his gravely voice to the Pakistani station manager. It sounded like he was saying, "Feely-ROPE-alo, PREE-mo."

Protecting himself from the artic wind that was blowing and shivering from head to toe, the attendant pulled his wool cap down to his ears and looked to me for help. I shrugged my shoulders, and he looked back over at Fajardo, who tried to clear things up.

"*Que lo filiropées, mi hermanito, 'Filiropeltan.' ¿O tú no underestán mai ingli, o qué? E'chale, primo.*"

Young Armandito read desperation in my face and came to our rescue. At that point the Pakistani and I learned that, translated from Fajardo Senior's special language, he had tried to say, "Fill 'er up" and that "primo"—cousin, in Spanish—had nothing to do with family relationships and meant that he wanted the tank filled with "premium."

"Well, that's what I said, isn't it? 'Feely-ROPE-alo, PREE-mo.' Am I speaking Chinese here?"

Armandito winked at me and smiled. After paying the confused Pakistani, we continued on our way to our matinée performance with the ineffable Fajardo and His Stars.

Another time, I was waiting for a famous American pianist to give me a ride to a gig at a jazz club in Wilmington, Delaware. At that time I was living with my folks in a neighborhood where almost everybody was either Cuban or from some other Spanish-speaking country. You hardly ever saw any Anglos in that part of Hudson County, New Jersey. (Still don't.)

"Hurry up, son! A foreigner named Tim McCoy is waiting for you," my mother told me as I was preparing for the gig.

"A foreigner named Tim McCoy, like that old cowboy in the silent movies?" I asked, mightily perplexed. "What are you talking about, Mom?"

When I got out to the living room, the foreigner was the great pianist McCoy Tyner, who had come to pick me up for that night's gig in Delaware. But never mind, everybody's got their problems. I've definitely encountered my own share of stumbling blocks when it comes to the English language. Like the time I was shopping with my wife at a Korean grocery store and I asked for a "rape avocado." The woman looked at me with disgust and answered, "You're sick."

"What?" I asked, a little frightened by the woman's tone of voice and fierce expression. Fortunately my wife spoke up, clarifying for the clerk that I was looking for a ripe avocado.

Pronunciation is a frustrating part of learning any language, especially when you find words that to the ear of a Spanish-speaker sound a lot like each other. For example, I prefer to say that I'm going "to the seashore" or "to the ocean," because "beach" is something completely different from "bitch." If I get it wrong and say "I'm going to the bitch," I'll sound like I'm going out for a wild night with prostitutes. Another example is "sheet," as in sheets for a bed or a sheet of paper, as opposed to "shit." That's why, in my profession, I always refer to "piano parts"; if I say "lead sheet" and it comes out "lead shit," God knows what kind of reaction I might get from American musicians.

Saying in English "Aunt Ann and an Ant" just sounds to us like someone trying to talk with his nose stuffed up. And you can imagine what a challenge it is to understand a language in which "ass" means "donkey" but also "butt." How the heck do you say *el culo del burro*, "the ass's ass"?

I am convinced that the most challenging part of a language is not speaking it, but understanding it, especially since, to make things even more complicated, there's the whole accent thing. One of my first experiences with strange accents was at the beginning of one of my first on-stage appearances with Dizzy Gillespie.

Dizzy was born in Cheraw, South Carolina, and we all know what those southern accents are like, don't we? Well, it was the opening night of Rock Head Paradise in Montreal. We were already on stage when I asked Dizzy what we were going to play. He answered with a noise that sounded like something between the underwater braying of a Cambodian buffalo and the snoring sound made by a diesel engine with compression problems.

I swallowed and asked Ed Cherry, the guitarist, who was next to me, "What did Gillespie say?"

"How the heck should I know?" he answered simply.

I insisted. "What do you mean you don't know? You're American, aren't you?"

"Yeah," he said. "But he's from South Carolina, and that's another planet, bro. Better wait till he starts to play, and you'll know right away where the shots are coming from."

He was right. And I learned once more that music—especially jazz—is the true universal language, the language of love, tolerance, and respect, free expression that flows between those who speak it and their audiences.

On the other hand, there is no doubt that, precisely due to its simplicity and practicality, the language of Shakespeare (or "Chah-Keh-SPEER-eh," as Martí liked to say) has become what people tried to create through Esperanto many years ago. That is to say, it has become a language that people of different latitudes can use to facilitate communication. On top of that, and despite the extreme difficulty some people may have understanding it, if we look at the subject with objectivity and optimism, you'd have to admit, my dear colleague Yeyito, things could have been a lot worse if we had had to break the frustrations of the language barrier in Cantonese, Urdu, or Bulgarian, don't you agree?

On the Road with Yo-Yo Ma

Confucius was one of the inventors of confusion. That's why he was one of the most ancient Chinese-Japanese men.
—Miss Panama 2009

You've probably noticed that in Cuba and all over Latin America, all Asians are referred to as Chinese or *chinos*, without anyone even checking out their place of birth. It's not a derogatory thing, just a bad habit. So much so, that the ex-president of Peru, Alberto Fujimori, is known among Peruvians as "El Chino Fujimori," and he doesn't complain about it at all.

Many years ago, during the Vietnam War, the state-controlled Cuban press constantly referred to the heroism of Vietnamese soldiers who tore down enemy planes with stones while Yankee imperialism raped old ladies and killed small children and defenseless animals (I can't remember in what order). Regular Cubans had to agree with the official line, and when referring to Ho Chi Minh they would say, "That Chinaman Ho is a tough guy. He keeps Americans on their toes."

I guess it's about the same here. Our talented young pianist Alex Brown told me a funny story about his grandfather in Maryland. Once in a parking lot, an Asian man rushed in before him and took the parking space he'd been waiting a few minutes to get into. Alex's grandfather yelled out, "Hey, where do you think you're going, Mr. Lee?" With his head halfway out the window the Asian man asked, "How did you know my name, sir?" It happens everywhere.

The great Brazilian trumpet player Cláudio Roditi and myself, have often called drummer Akira Tana "Akira the Chinaman." But Akira is very Japanese. It also happens in my own family with my aunt Esperanza, whom we call mulatta, a mixed race black woman, as of the family's nine brothers and sisters, she's the darkest. Aunt Esperanza had a Korean husband and we all called him Mao Tse Tung. Since he was a communist at heart, he didn't mind being nicknamed after the Chinese dictator. His real name was Alberto, a name that has nothing to do with China, Korea, or any Asian country.

Brazil has one of the largest Japanese communities outside of Japan, but they also call people with oblique eyes and very dark straight hair "Chinamen." That's probably why, of all the musicians that had the pleasure of recording and traveling the world to promote cellist Yo-Yo Ma's record *Obrigado Brazil*, it was the Assad brothers and me that called Yo-Yo "Chino" for the first time. The extraordinary artist was born in Paris, to Chinese parents, both music teachers whose illustrious son is the best evidence of their educational abilities.

Sérgio and Odair Assad, the sui generis Brazilian guitar duo, and I concur that Ma is the best-educated, well-mannered man we've found in this world. I am positive that the rest of the troupe agrees. Five Brazilians, a British pianist, and a Cuban clarinetist (yours truly) formed the group that toured from Amsterdam to Taipei to Japan, Germany, and the USA. I asked Yo-Yo to dedicate the concert at the colossal Hollywood Bowl of Los Angeles in front of an audience of seventeen thousand people to the memory of Celia Cruz, who had left us earlier that month. It was probably the first time in history that a classical artist dedicated his show to a *guarachera*.

On another occasion and as interesting trivia, Yo-Yo Ma presented our performances in the Land of the Rising Sun totally in Japanese, using Chinese alphabet cards and reading words phonetically in a language he later told me was totally unknown to him.

As was expected, the Brazilian album won a Grammy in 2003 and as a result of the tremendous success of that tour, Sony decided to produce *Obrigado Brazil: Volume II*, recorded live in New York's Zankel Hall. This time the eclectic repertoire included compositions by Sérgio Assad, Antônio Carlos Jobim, Egberto Gismonti, Astor Piazzolla, Ary Barroso, Jacob do Bandolim, César Camargo Mariano, and my "Afro" piece, a modest tribute to Africa's huge contribution to the music of the New World. On the same album, my piece "Merengue," based on an exotic 5/4 Venezuelan rhythm, won me another Grammy for best instrumental composition. In addition to the Assad brothers and Kathryn Stott's piano, Nilson Matta's bass, and Cyro Baptista's percussion, we had the crystalline voice of Rosa Passos.

As well as a great musician El Chino Yo-Yo is a fun guy, especially in the after-concert dinners. There was a time in Hong Kong, when they made reservations for the whole group to dine in a luxurious restaurant in the city. While we were all seated, Yo-Yo unexpectedly came through the kitchen's swinging doors, wearing his black slacks and white shirt, a white napkin folded on his right forearm, a bottle of French wine in the opposite hand. He served all of us with a smile from one ear to the other. Then he grabbed a fresh bottle from a wine rack that held many bottles and greeted everyone in the room. He served wine in every empty glass he found. Everyone in the restaurant drank from that wine, even people we had never seen in our lives and had nothing to do with our group.

I got up to sneak around the area and get a breath of fresh air when an American guy leaving the restaurant said, "That waiter who looks like Yo-Yo Ma was odd, man. First he filled everyone's glass with wine that no one asked for. Then, he has the nerve to sit at your table and eat all the food. Truly there are guys that'll do anything! Amazing, isn't it?"

Shark

Viva, Viva. The Madmen who invented Love!
—"Ballad for a Madman" by Horacio Ferrer and Astor
Piazzolla

Some people are born to be creative, original, and different, although often in their lives they find themselves misunderstood and attacked by their peers. That was the case for Beethoven, Charlie Parker, Stravinsky, and Astor Piazzolla, a man who, when not making music, flew to Punta del Este to hunt sharks only to return them to the sea. I've often heard his grandson, drummer Daniel "Pipi" Piazzolla, talk enthusiastically about his marine adventures with his grandfather.

Astor must have inherited his fishing hobby from his paternal grandfather Pantaleón, an Italian seaman that emigrated with his family at the end of the nineteenth century from the port of Trani in the southeast of Italy to Mar del Plata, Argentina. That's where Astor was born in 1921. In 1925 he moved with his parents to Greenwich Village in New York City, a diverse working-class neighborhood that also housed part of the underworld. It was in those tough and violent streets of the Village that Astor learned self-defense and to fight hard even though he walked with a limp.

At the Piazzolla home they heard Gardel and other tango masters. Astor was exposed to jazz and classical music—mainly Bach, who definitely marked him. In 1929, his dad, the immortal "Nonino," gave him a *bandoneon* he bought in a pawnshop. Years later, with his creativity and vision, and against the opinion of many "purists," the only son of Vicente and Asunta totally changed the musical landscape of his country of origin. Since time heals all wounds, no one remembers now they used to call him the "tango's assassin."

In 1934 he met the foremost tango singer, Carlos Gardel, and even had a small role in one his movies, *El día que quieras*. Gardel invited him to join in a South American tour, but Nonino didn't give the thirteen-year-old permission to go on the road. And that was precisely the tour on which Gardel's June 25, 1935 flight from Medellín, Colombia crashed. It wasn't meant for Astor to leave us yet. "If my old man would have let me go on tour, I'd be playing harp on a cloud today and not the bandoneon," jokes Astor.

Astor had a very dark sense of humor, which we attribute to those who have a penchant for playing pranks in bad taste. But he didn't at all like to be on the receiving end, and that is where he and I clashed. Whenever he played one on me, I ripped back with an even worse one, and things went downhill from there.

Thus began the pleasant telephone conversation I had with Fernando Suárez Paz, the exquisite violinist from Buenos Aires who was by Astor Piazzolla's side during the last eleven years of his life. "El Negro," as his colleagues affectionately call him, isn't black at all. He's a tall, solid man, rather serious. Olive-skinned and dreamy-eyed, with the features of an Araucan chieftain or something like it. If someone asked me for the definition of soul, expression, and feeling for playing a musical instrument, his name would immediately come to mind. I never heard anyone else play the vibrato in such an emotional and effective way.

"The little streets of Buenos Aires have that... I don't know what..." go Horacio Ferrer's lyrics in the introduction to his immortal "Ballad for a Madman," with music by Piazzolla. That *je ne sais quoi* one undoubtedly feels walking through the lively streets of the Argentinean capital, with its hundreds of pizzerias, outdoor cafes, green parks, and massive marble monuments reminiscent of the old continent. An ample and healthy capital, a combination of Spain, Italy, and slum tango, or *tango arrabalero*, a musical genre born to a mother from Havana and father from Buenos Aires with an African name.

The tango adopted the bandoneón, a Germanic accordion-like instrument no longer in use, devilishly difficult to play, and, on top of that, no longer manufactured, since the only factory that made them was destroyed during World War II. The only way to carry on the tradition is repairing the existing ones.

Although without the dazzling beauty of Paris or New York, there is no doubting the particular charms of Buenos Aires, with its aroma of brewed *mate* and barbecued meats, and the sad lyrics about inmates and love betrayed in its *milonga*, the dance music from the Rio de la Plata region. The strumming of the guitars coming from the *boliches*, or nightclubs, and the insinuating walks of its beautiful women make the city a unique experience that calls for living life to the fullest.

Buenos Aires is the birthplace of great writers, poets, singers, composers, and musicians. In that romantic city, Jorge Luis Borges was born. Also born there, on January 1, 1941, was Fernando Suárez Paz. Thirty-seven years later he would meet Astor Piazzolla, with whom he traveled around the world non-stop and recorded eighteen albums and innumerable movie soundtracks. In 2003, during a concert with his own quintet in the majestic Teatro Colón, the legendary violinist was named Most Illustrious Citizen by the City of Buenos Aires.

In the fall of 1987, I saw him play in Manhattan for the first time, at a place on Seventh Avenue south called SOB's, as a member of Astor Piazzolla's Nuevo Tango Quintet. The pianist was the charismatic Pablo Ziegler, who joined the group a little before El Negro. At that time I had been recording some tracks from Piazzolla's latest album for Kip Hanrahan's label American Clavé. For some reason, neither Ziegler nor Astor's bassist were able to do the New York session, and that is when Piazzolla himself asked the Uruguayan Pablo Singer, who lived in New York and was often mistaken for his Argentinean colleague Pablo Ziegler, to co-produce, play piano, and organize the entire repertoire of *Tango Apasionado*, which was the title of the album. Piazzolla, who didn't know the Uruguayan personally, called him on the phone at his New York apartment, near the tomb of Ulysses S. Grant in the Big Apple.

"Hello, may I please speak with Pablo Singer?"

"Speaking," said Pablo.

"This is Astor Piazzolla, and I wanted to know if you'd be able to take on the direction of my next musical production in New York?"

"Get outta here, who's this?" Pablo replied incredulously.

"It is really Astor Piazzolla," Piazzolla said.

"Oof," Pablo answered, realizing it was true. "Sorry, Maestro!"

When they cleared the air, they called me in to play a few pieces, rounding out the group made up of Astor, Pablo, Rodolfo Alchurrón on electric guitar, and, as double-bassist, the versatile Andy González. Andy played that session as if he'd been born in San Telmo on the Port of Rio de la Plata instead of in the Bronx. The combo's vedette (as Astor called him) was once again the incredible "Negro" Suárez Paz, casting a musical spell with his passionate violin.

Years later, when I asked El Negro to tell me about his association with the man who forever changed the face of the tango, there was a long and deep sigh at the other end of the line, followed by a very mischievous peal of laughter.

"When he called me on the phone to ask me to join his quintet in 1978, he said to me, 'Play close attention to my proposal; the violin is the vedette of the group.'

"'Then do I have to play it naked?' I said. 'I've heard you were a bit of a joker, but I wish to make it very clear that I'm in earnest. I was also warned about your pranks. But tell me, why don't we talk about the music? After all, you called me to play, right? So that is what I'm willing to do.'"

And that's how the story goes about Astor and El Negro, who had already wielded his mighty musical weapons against the first violins of the National Symphony of Argentina and the Buenos Aires Philharmonic, and played under batons of the likes of Lalo Schifrin, Burt Bacharach, Waldo de los Ríos, and Michel Legrand. In the genre of the tango he played alongside Horacio Salgán, Mariano Mores, Nestor Marconi, the historic Sexteto Mayor, Aníbal Troilo, and other emblematic figures.

This violinist, who is highly regarded and much loved among his colleagues, has a very peculiar sense of humor, sharp and dry as a slug of Dutch gin.

During the two days of the concerts in Buenos Aires, Piazzolla got very stressed over schedules. He always wanted to have everything ready two hours early, and when I arrived two hours early, he said to me, "Why are you late?"

"Because I'm coming from a recording session where we played three of your songs," I answered. "And besides, I'm not late, I'm early."

"What did you record and with whom?" he asked.

I answered him, but I won't name names here. Among the three pieces was the theme "Contratiempo."

"Very good," he said. "And how does 'Contratiempo' go?"

"What the hell do I know, man?" I said. "All your stuff sounds the same!"

He was stunned; nobody had ever talked to him like that. That is how our friendship began. The next day, when they said my name, he grabbed me by the jacket and, pulling me hard, let me go just as we went up on stage... I almost fell. Well, during the intermission I took all the music sheets on his stand and turned them upside down. I avenged myself and we were even.

In their excellent Pizzollian bio Susana Azzi and Simon Collier wrote, "The intense rhythm of the trips in 1986 set the bar for the rest of the decade." The tours lasted a little less than a month and included seventeen or eighteen concerts. It was pretty heavy and created a lot of tension. Astor's obsession with punctuality became markedly worse with time, and he gave the musicians who were late to the airport a lot of grief.

It was a time of heavy drug trafficking in Europe, much of it smuggled by South Americans. On one occasion, customs officials at the Munich Airport took Fernando Suárez Paz off to a private office and made him strip down to his underwear. The rest of the musicians had no inkling about the whereabouts of the violinist and began to look for him all over the terminal. As a gesture of defiance, El Negro took off what little clothes he was wearing, and while authorities went through his belongings, he picked up his instrument and began to play "Meditation," the sublime violin solo from the opera *Thaïs* by Massenet. Upon hearing the violin, Astor found the door, opened it, and burst out laughing. He was almost rolling on the floor. The cops told him to shut up, because they wanted to listen to the music.

"I kept on playing naked for the longest time, and when I finished, the officers began applauding, teary-eyed," Suárez Paz said.

Astor Piazolla was born in Mar del Plata on March 11, 1921. When he was four, he migrated with his parents to New York. He went to school for the first time there in 1926, and in those formative years he picked up that peculiar American accent he carried throughout his life. When he turned eight, his father gave him an accordion, and by the age of nine, he returned with his family to Mar del Plata. Years later, misunderstood and frequently attacked on account of his innovative musical tendencies, he went into exile in Europe.

Among many other pieces he wrote the monumental "Concierto de Nácar" (Ivory Concert) for violin and orchestra, dedicated to Fernando Suárez Paz. After a prolonged illness, the life of the author of "Adios Nonino" was finally extinguished on July 4, 1992 in Buenos Aires, where he was finally accepted and revered as one of the greatest artists of all time.

On various occasions, in different parts of the world, groups were assembled to play his music, and they did it with the best of intentions, but Astor's music is incredibly difficult to play the way it was meant to be played. The problem was that the music was born from the tango, and the tango, in order to really swing, has to be played backwards from what the music indicates.

Once he said to Suárez Paz, "Negro, when I'm no longer on this planet, I leave you in charge of my music so that it lives on the same way it was born."

In 1996, Fernando Suárez Paz headed a quintet in the fashion of that chamber group of Piazzolla's, solely devoted to interpreting the works of the great Argentinean composer. They played concerts in Israel, Portugal, Spain, the US, Brazil, and Uruguay. He recorded two albums with this group: *Milonga del Ángel* and *Por Amor a Astor*.

Another time, showing his appreciation, he wrote a theme for El Negro, "Escuchalo." He wrote it in a rhythm that isn't *candombe* or *milonga*, neither African nor Rio de la Plata dance; it was something very original and fierce.

When he brought it to Suárez Paz, he said, "Listen to me, Negro, I've written this for you. Now play it, if you can. It's beautiful; you must have heard it," he added ironically.

"Paquito," he would later tell me, "that is how we spent eleven years of our lives, filled with joy, and best of all, making his beautiful music. So when they asked me to join the quintet to play his pieces, I joined it with all my love."

Brazil

Meu Brasil brasileiro, Terra de Samba e Pandeiro.
—Ary Barroso

Yeyito, I think I might have mentioned this somewhere else. I don't know about you, but when we Cubans want to authenticate something, we declare, "Martí said it." They also say that Martí once declared, "If I wasn't Cuban, I'd like to be one." But experts assure me he never said it. He would have liked to have said it... I think. Because it's a good phrase, and it goes well with the natural Cuban pride of being who we are. I myself say it every time Bebo Valdés or Albita win a Grammy, or when Carlos Alberto Montaner writes one of his super articles, or any time a *cubiche* does something meritorious.

That phrase would work just fine for Brazilians too. They have a giant country, with a gigantic culture and a natural splendor I haven't found anywhere else in the world. I have met tons of Brazilian experts all over the planet who understand the language and know the food and music of Brazil as if they were born there. One of them is my friend, the singer Estrella da Costa, whom I met in the early '80s singing bossa novas and *falando português* with Cláudio Roditi. Her real name is Estrella Acosta, and she is from San José de los Ramos, Cuba, the same town where pianist composer Fernando Mulens was born.

For many years now, I have had the greatest affinity for Brazilians. That's why, for Mother's Day, I gave my mom a trip to Rio de Janeiro with Carmen, my beloved mother-in-law. Awaiting them in Brazil were no other than Gladys, Cláudio Roditi's mother (rest in peace), and our old friend the small giant Leny Andrade, first lady of Brazilian jazz.

The initial problem was Carioca hospitality. Soon after the ladies got off the plane, a handsome suntanned Brazilian male approached them with a welcoming glass of cachaça. He smiled at them and said, *"Bem-vindas ao Brasil, vocês gostam de uma Pinga?"*

But, to a couple of Caribbean ladies pushing sixty, that last word, though tempting, was a bit too strong. Leny then explained that they shouldn't think anything of it, because although in Caribbean Spanish, the word has an (almost) unacceptable sexual connotation, in the delightful language of the Cariocas, it only describes a sweet alcoholic beverage that if consumed in moderation is totally inoffensive.

Brazilians are a people of never-ending charm, and as singer-guitarist Trini Márquez told me once, they have a mixture of joyful sorrow or sorrowful joy in their music as no other culture has. They have achieved the most perfect balance between rhythm, harmony, melody, and lyrics in the world. That's why I admire Antônio Carlos Brasileiro de Almeida Jobim so very much. To earn such a special place in the heart of a community of composers is indeed a double honor.

Jobim said, "Life in the United States is wonderful, but it's shitty, and life in Brazil is shitty, but it's wonderful."

Now, you interpret that however you like, but to me it seems most creative, like everything about him. Once BMI threw a birthday party for Jobim and gathered a distinguished group of composers that included Manny Albam, Gerry Mulligan, Michel Camilo, Perico Ortiz, and Roger Kellaway (whom Jobim kept calling Cab Calloway). Tom (as the Carioca musician was nicknamed) complained that in Brazil he was robbed and cheated of his music rights and that's why he joined BMI. That afternoon they had brought in a magnificent Steinway grand piano, where the author of "Wave" sat and played most of the time.

It was the perfect occasion for me to ask him about the harmony and melody of bars thirteen and fourteen of the main theme, his beautiful song "Corcovado," which everyone plays in a different way. Tom, with his usual circumspection, played the passage that so intrigued me one way and another. After a few minutes he lifted his eyes from the piano and, with a mischievous smile, pointed to the president of the society and answered, "Bah! Play it whichever way you want. These gringos pay me anyway..."

Antônio Carlos Jobim, the man that Rio de Janeiro's International Airport was named after, was that amusing and unprompted.

The good thing about New York City is the amount of people from all over the world that live in it. The Brazilian community is massive here, and I've made friends with many of them since I arrived in New York thirty-five years ago. I've been able to learn a lot from the Brazilian culture, which I have loved from the time I was a child and heard my father play on his tenor saxophone Zequinha de Abreu's *chorinho* "Tico-Tico no Fubá."

Amid the Brazilians I met here is percussionist Cyro Baptista, who has a group called Beat the Donkey. We have recorded with Yo-Yo Ma and other great artists several times. Cyro always has a funny story to tell. Once he told me that after living in New York a few years, he went to visit his father in Brazil. His dad was a serious, conservative man that didn't like at all an earring Cyro was wearing on the left ear. Mr. Baptista was silent for a long time looking indiscreetly at his son's earring.

"So, what about that earring?" he asked. "Pirate or faggot?"

My first trip to Brazil was in 1985 or '86, after finishing a week with my quintet at the Satchmo Jazz Club in Lima, Peru. From Chabuca Granda and César Vallejo's land we went to do another week at the luxurious Maksoud Plaza Hotel in São Paulo. We had Cláudio Roditi on trumpet, Sergio Brandão on bass guitar, Michel Camilo on piano, and on drums the dynamic Portinho, who hadn't been back to Brazil in eighteen years. At the Maksoud's piano bar I met the tiny and talented pianist, composer, and singer Johnny Alf. They said that he was already doing bossa nova before he invented the name.

Cuban and Brazilian food have one point of convergence: rice and beans (*feijão*). Not avocado, though. While we eat it in salads, they make shakes and ice cream with it. That's something crazy for Caribbean people. A typical Cuban joke is to order avocado ice cream. It's almost like asking for chicken custard (flan) or a green olive shake with condensed milk and onions.

The interesting thing is that in Brazil no one orders beans in a restaurant, and much less in a luxury outfit like the Maksoud Plaza. I did it, and with a laugh, they explained that except Thursdays, which is the *feijoada completa* in many restaurants, beans are only eaten at home. I was so surprised when the next day (and without me even ordering it), the waiter brought me a bowl of navy beans, white rice, and a sliced avocado seasoned with olive oil and vinegar. Upon seeing my astonished face, the man pointed at the kitchen entrance. A middle-aged mulatta with a yellow scarf on her head, who looked like my aunt Delia, smiled timidly with an indescribable sweetness. She waved a greeting at me.

"The lady heard our conversation yesterday, and today she wanted to share with you the beans she brought for her own lunch," said the waiter in Portuñol. "The avocado salad is courtesy of the house, Don Paquito," he added with reverence.

After that time, I've been back many times to that amazing, magic land, blessed and undoubtedly touched by the hand of God. I have had the immense pleasure of sharing the stage and recording studio with many of Brazil's remarkable classical, popular, and jazz musicians, from César Camargo Mariano, Gustavo Tavares, the Zimbo Trio, and the amazingly fabulous Assad brothers to Rosa Passos, Romero Lubambo, the Trio Corrente, and the unbelievable Nailor "Proveta" Azevedo with his Banda Mantiqueira. (In 2014, I even won a Grammy and a Latin Grammy back-to-back for my song with Trio Corrente, "Song For Maura," dedicated to my beloved mother.)

My love for Brazil, Brazilians, and their extremely rich culture has often made me say that even though I am proud of being Cuban and for having been born and raised in José

Martí and Ernesto Lecuona's fatherland, half of *meu coração é brasileiro*.

Through the years, that affection seems to have been mutual. I have always felt accepted by Brazilians and always felt I am part of their fascinating tuneful world. So much that when Yo-Yo Ma recorded *Obrigado Brazil: Volumes I and II*, I was the chosen clarinetist along with Rosa Passos, the Assad brothers, Nilson Matta, and a whole clan of wonderful Cariocas, Amazonians, Northeasterners, and Paulistas.

Some people even think I am Carioca, and when Chicano actor Edward James Olmos shot his impactful documentary *Americanos*, I was commissioned to organize the Brazilian segment. I surrounded myself with a distinguished group of musicians from the land of Heitor Villa-Lobos: Sergio Brandão on bass and cavaquinho, Portinho on drums and percussion, and Romero Lubambo on guitar (or *violão*, as they call it), all accompanied by an excellent symphonic orchestra that Olmos hired for the special occasion.

The repertory I chose for the TV show with Gloria Estéfan, Tito Puente, Linda Ronstadt, and many other music celebrities was precisely "Tico-Tico no Fubá" and my "Samba to Brenda with Love." I closed, as I often do, saying "Sebastian Bach was really a Carioca, and his real name was João Sebastião Bach." It always works in making people laugh.

For more than three decades, my band's musical theme has been Maurício Einhorn's and Durval Ferreira's "Estamos Aí." Since I heard it for the first time in the late '60s at the home of model Norka Méndez, it bewitched me. I remember it was a live recording of the Brazilian group Gemini Cinco, a combination of the Bossa Tres trio and singers Pery Ribeiro and

Leny Andrade. Those who are familiar with my discography or have been at my concerts know that composers like Tom Jobim, Hermeto Pascoal, Heitor Villa-Lobos, Pixinguinha, and Roditi are always present in my performances.

A great deal of my repertory includes sambas, bossa novas, *baiãos*, *frevos*, and other Brazilian musical genres. I have always maintained that it's not necessary to be born in Austria to play Mozart. Only talent, dedication, and respect for each musical genre are a must. That's why Mark Walker, Diego Urcola, Alex Brown, Pernell Saturnino, Pedrito Martínez, Oscar Stagnaro, and all my non-Brazilian musicians (some of them have been with me over twenty years) are so confident and at ease with those styles.

Before I finish this Brazilian chapter, I can't leave out a story told to me by Argentine composer Lalo Schiffrin about a great Brazilian singer.

Maysa Matarazzo was married to the Count of Matarazzo, who had an awful reputation. They called him the Marquis de Sade of Brazil. There were rumors that he corrupted Maysa, exposing her to all sorts of sexual perversions. I never pay attention to rumors, and since she wanted to meet record producers and film directors, I threw a dinner party for her at my home. I invited Jack Lemmon, Peter Falk, Stuart Rosenberg, and other Hollywood VIPs. Almost all of them came with their wives. Since we had a good social and musical relationship, I also invited Ray Brown. After dinner we all gathered in the living room. By that time Maysa Matarazzo was so drunk that not only couldn't she sing, but she started to pose seductively and flirt with the men... and their wives too!

"Come now, let's go to the bathroom and do *pipi* together," she said.

I have never been so embarrassed in my life, but the incident didn't affect my love for Brazil and its music. Poor Lalo! Above all I felt bad for his wife Donna. Although in reality I won't deny that I thought the whole thing was hysterical. That's why I include it here. Besides, as Pedro Flores's *guaracha* sung by the Márquez Sisters says, "*Borracho no vale,*" or "It doesn't count if you're drunk." Isn't that the truth?

Latin Jazz, the Musical Interpretation of Spanglish

Jazz: Americano nigger-kike jungle music.
—Joseph Goebbels

One cold winter morning I was jamming with my friend, Argentinian saxophonist Oscar Feldman, inside a hotel ballroom in the outskirts of New York. Feldman's presentation with me as a special guest was part of an event to promote a music school. There were many middle-and high-school-level teachers in the audience. At the end of the show, an older lady, apparently a member of the teacher caucus, came towards us. Her demeanor was fragile and severe at the same time, like a professor's. Her hair was pulled in a chignon. Thick, somewhat old-fashioned, horn-rimmed eyeglasses rested on her nose, and a wooden walking cane hung from her right arm. She was interested in acquiring a copy of the last piece we played, apparently for a school group to practice on.

The piece was Duke Ellington's "I Let a Song Go Out of My Heart." It was arranged and re-harmonized by Oscar, who immediately gave her a copy of the piano part we used as a guide to improvise. The part was simple and small, with the melody, chords, and some rhythmic effects Oscar added to Ellington's composition. She gave the paper a long distrustful look, as if Oscar were trying to play some kind of a joke she couldn't understand. The old lady frowned, took the heavy eyeglasses off, smoothed her hair, and stared at us one by one. She finally said, "As I can read music, I recognize parts of the melody you played on this *little* paper, but what I'd like to know is, where in hell are the other ten minutes I heard written?"

After a brief silence, we looked at each other and let out a big laugh. I left with the other musicians, leaving Oscar Feldman there, trying to explain to the classical music teacher what he understands as "the Miracle Lead Sheet." What happens is that for those who have strictly classical music training, it's very difficult to understand how those who improvise can play more or less coherently for a long time without reading music parts.

Misunderstood and discriminated against since birth, it has taken time for jazz and its players to be accepted and respected, even in the country where the genre was born. Even today, we find students that think Louis Armstrong was the first man that walked on the moon. Even on the other side of American borders, the controversial genre has caused political problems for those who love it around the world.

Adolf Hitler's ideologists created a ten-commandment code where they even limited the percentage of authorized syncopated rhythms. Germans could only use ten percent of them in their compositions and musical arrangements. That way they could differentiate "disgusting Black-Judeo music" or "American jungle music," as Joseph Goebbels liked to call it, from pure German music lightly flavored by jazzy touches.

What was totally contradictory was that the Führer's secretary of propaganda was not only a fervent admirer of jazz but also the owner of the largest record collection in the Third Reich. The similarity of subjective rules reminds me of the Cuban Gray Quinquennial (or "gray five year period"), when a power-abusing member of the Cuban military named Papito Serguera persecuted "Satanic" love songs, tangos, and boleros with sad lyrics. According to him they didn't represent the joy of living that should inspire revolutions. Serguera was the director of the ICRT (Cuban Institute of Radio and Television). One of the first examples of binding happy love songs was given by composer Alberto Vera, a senior official of the institute, when Omara Portuondo recorded "Lo que me queda por vivir" ("What is left of my life to live"), a mediocre copy of the classic love song "Sabor a mi," composed by Alvaro Carrillo from Mexico.

It's not a coincidence that Hitler's second "commandment" of the ten his cultural hygienists invented suggested the preference of high tones and lyrics that expressed happiness instead of "dark Jewish lyrics."

In 1943, member of the resistance Leopold Tyrmand, a Polish Jew, was sent to a forced labor camp in Frankfurt, Germany. Forty years later, Tyrmand returned to that same city as an accomplished writer, president of the Rockford Institute. He was a speaker in the conference "On Freedom." There, he pronounced one of the most beautiful and moving definitions of jazz:

In times of Nazi barbarism, jazz became for us a system of latitudes subjected to a freely accepted discipline of principal links between the individual and a group. As such, this is probably the best metaphor on freedom anyone could create. It entails the message that there is a central authority, usually holding a trumpet, to which each person is responsible for maintaining correct tones and timing.

At the same time, they each have a turn for the right to a fair equitable space for individual expression. This is exactly what constitutes the basic principle from which a series of liberties emerge. It becomes a perfect allegory to the many opportunities in it so that anyone that can play an instrument and contributes to the common sound can in his own way declare what they find beautiful and real. To me particularly, this music makes me think of free people. Don't ask me why!

That sensation of independence seems to be exactly the reason that totalitarian leaders (it doesn't matter if they are communists, Nazis, or Islamic fundamentalists) are so afraid of jazz musicians. On the other side of the ideological frontier, around 1962, the Soviet Premier Nikita Khrushchev publicly declared he didn't like jazz and when by accident he listened to it on the radio, he confused it with the sound of static. "What balls!" Argentine musicians would say. (Although even at this point, some of them still admire that shitty political system.)

"Malignant begot product of the decaying occidental society" was Mao Tse Tung's best definition of this fascinating musical expression. When his troops captured Shanghai in

1948, its dynamic nightlife was terminated simply because they considered the jazz clubs "decadent" and incompatible with socialism. Twenty-two years later, Fidel Castro's chosen troglodyte José Llanuza used a similar argument to close our "polluted imperialist music vice dens."

The rest is history. Perhaps I should have said "hysterics."

Yet, there's always someone more messed up than you. The Taliban, for example, forbids music… all music, period! From mambo and Viennese waltzes to reggaeton and heavy metal (not all bad after all). There were no movies or leisure TV either, and women were hidden under the "burka" and didn't wear deodorant! The only amusement they left for men were camel races and the ball to kick—and that's when they didn't have public executions at soccer stadiums. Believe it or not, even flying kites was forbidden, and that's the national pastime in Afghanistan. Poor Afghans. Shit! No beer, no TV, no women, no music, and no kites! If gringos didn't come to their rescue, they'd still be praying five times a day and fucking goats in Kabul and Kandahar.

In the early '90s Marc Crawford wrote an excellent essay, "Hitler's Failed Intention of Destroying Jazz in Europe." In the essay the author mentions Freddy Johnson, an Afro-American pianist that had played the best jazz places in Europe since 1928. Benny Carter was also there, and he recorded around fifty albums with Coleman Hawkins. In December 1941, the Gestapo came looking for Johnson three days after the US declared war on Japan. They sent him to a concentration camp in Bavaria along with Afro-American singer Valaida Snow. On March 1944 they exchanged him for some German prisoners and returned to New York.

Freddy Johnson was probably the most recognized jazz musician in Amsterdam when occupying Nazi troops arrived. That gorgeous city had a jazz club called La Cubana where his trio played every night. The fact that a North American musician had a club named "La Cubana" in Amsterdam in the 1930s confirms the strong ties between jazz and Cuban and Latin music in general, since its beginnings. It's a natural reflection of the multicultural and multinational American society and the monumental Latino contribution to the language of jazz.

Since the early twentieth century, legendary pianist composer Jelly Roll Morton spoke about what he called the "Hispanic touch in American music." Since then, names like Manuel Pérez, Alberto Socarrás, Tito Puente, Arturo "Chico" O'Farrill, Emiliano Salvador, Luiz Bonfá, Fats Navarro, Lalo Schifrin, Ray Barretto, Cachao, Antônio Carlos Jobim, Dave Valentín, Bebo and Chucho Valdés, Cláudio Roditi, Astor Piazzolla, Michel Camilo, and many others have been of crucial relevance to each period of jazz.

Born in Manzanillo, Cuba on September 18, 1908, Alberto Socarrás passed away in New York on August 26, 1987. It was Socarrás who recorded the first ever flute solo in the piece "Have You Ever Felt That Way?" with the Clarence Williams Orchestra on February 5, 1929.

The Puerto Rican trombonist Juan Tizol substantially contributed to Duke Ellington's Orchestra's repertory, while Mario Bauzá was indispensable in the beginning of Ella Fitzgerald's career. It was he that introduced Ella to Chick Webb in the 1930s. Later on, Mario put Dizzy Gillespie in contact with Chano Pozo and Chico O'Farrill.

That association developed into what was known then as "Cubop," precursor of today's Latin jazz. In my humble opinion it is the true musical interpretation of the "Spanglish" we all speak now.

The Guitar

My dear Yeyito, though I don't know exactly where you are from, I am sure that if you live outside the homeland, the strum of guitar strings will bring you sad or happy memories of your town, because there isn't a more universal and catalytic instrument than the guitar.

Atahualpa Yupanqui wrote, "I walk through the world, I am poor, and I have nothing, just a warm heart and a passion: the guitar."

Andrés Segovia used to say that a guitar is a small orchestra; each string is a color, a different voice. He thought that among God's creatures, there were only two that came in every size and form not to ever be separated from man: the dog and the guitar. He recommended that his students move their bodies lightly forward to support the guitar with their chest. "Music's poetry must resonate in your hearts," he affirmed.

As long as the guitar has traveled in the arms of troubadours and minstrels of the six continents and through time and space, it's been the most practical and versatile instrument in the world, serving popular singers, classical composers, blues and jazz musicians, rock-and-rollers, *boleristas,* *soneros* from Cuba's Oriente, serenaders in Mexico, Spain, and

Portugal, *serenatas y parrandas* in Puerto Rico, and *rodas de choro* in Rio de Janeiro. The noble instrument that served as expressive vehicle for such diverse artists as Francisco Tárrega, Django Reinhardt, Paco de Lucía, Charlie Christian, and the Van Halen brothers has had a constant and robust presence in Latin American pop music. The sensual beauty of the melodies and rhythms of Cuba, Brazil, Paraguay, Argentina, and Venezuela had a huge power of attraction over composers and interpreters of academic formation like Heitor Villa-Lobos, Antonio Lauro, the brothers Sérgio and Odair Assad, Ruben and Rodrigo Riera, Flores Chaviano, Alirio Díaz, Leo Brouwer, and Rey Guerra, just to mention a few.

Among all these renowned Latin American artists, the name of illustrious Agustín Pío Barrios Mangoré, Paraguayan composer and virtuoso guitarist, who, in the opinions of many, invented the art of classical guitar in Latin America and whom Villa-Lobos, in a frenzy of uncontainable admiration, called "The Unreachable."

In addition to the Ellington and Benny Goodman records my father constantly played in his stereo, I was also exposed through national radio in my conservatory days to the captivating cadence of Guaraní music, in its original form and in creative adaptations that Orquesta Aragón and other groups brought with grace and mischief to Cuban rhythms.

I had been a loyal admirer for many years of the exquisite art of Berta Rojas when the extraordinary Paraguayan guitarist invited me to accompany her in a tribute to Mangoré with the master's music along with other distinguished Latin American composers and arrangers. I felt as excited as I would have been if Charlie Christian invited me to play and record all of Ellington's music. Berta is one of the most celebrated figures in the guitar scene today. She was praised by the *Washington Post* as guitarist extraordinaire. She played at Carnegie Hall, the Frederick P. Rose Jazz Hall, at the Lincoln Center in New York, at the Kennedy Center in Washington, DC, and in Dublin's National Concert Hall. Recently, she was a soloist of the Brussels Philharmonic Orchestra at Flagey's Studio 4 in Brussels, in a concert for Belgian National Television. Her *Intimate Barrios* CD is one of the most celebrated recordings of the works of great composer and guitarist Agustin Barrios. With the *Cielo Abierto* (Open Sky) and *Terruño* (Homeland) CD's she achieved great critics' recognition, and she has recorded the *Alma y Corazón* (Heart and Soul) CD with Carlos Barbosa Lima. She was artistic director of the four editions of the Ibero-American Guitar Festival at the Smithsonian Museum in Washington, DC and co-founder of the Beatty Competition and the Cardozo Ocampo Award to launch the careers of young artists. Her teachers were Felipe Sosa, Violeta de Mestral, and Abel Carlevaro. She received her BA in Music from the the Escuela Universitaria de Música in Uruguay, where she was a student of Eduardo Fernández and Mario Payseé. She achieved a Masters in Music at the Peabody Institute, under the guidance of Manuel Barrueco. She was selected as Kennedy Center for the Performing Arts' Fellow of the Americas for her artistic excellence. She is an Ambassador of Paraguay's Tourism and is actually a professor and chair of guitar at George Washington University. As you leave Asunción, entering the airport, you see a huge billboard with Berta and her guitar on stage. She is a true national treasure in her country.

Our joint album was recorded in the basement of the home of Oscar and Nury Serafini, a charming Paraguayan couple that have adopted Berta in their beautiful home in the outskirts of Washington. During the days we enjoyed the Serafini hospitality, *chipas* (delicious bread), and other exquisite Guaraní dishes, and got in the mood for our repertoire.

This is what writer Mario Rubén Alvarez wrote on the inside cover of the record about our project and my short stay in Asunción:

> *Time for the Guaraní, the original inhabitants of Paraguay, was an ample space that held diverse manifestations of life. They ignored the Western division of the day into hours. Pyhareve, in Guaraní, is the morning; asaje, the siesta; and ka'aru, the afternoon.*
>
> *When Paquito D'Rivera was coming to Paraguay to play in a concert with Berta Rojas last year, he said a day and a half was not enough to see, listen to, and feel Paraguay. Without knowing the Paraguayan culture, still with many components of Guaraní in daily life, beginning with the Indian language that is spoken here, which seventy-five percent of the population understands, he used a thought matrix typical of the land that was about to welcome him. That's why he didn't mention the thirty-six hours of permanence.*
>
> *In that brief day and a half, he lived the essence of our people—our cordiality, our love of music, our solidarity, and our respect for artists. The synthesis of that warm and affectionate meeting was Berta and Paquito's concert at the Bank of Paraguay's theater.*

The harmony of that unforgettable night wasn't only about two instrumentalists that recreated a repertory made to the image and semblance of their own virtuosity, but of a pair of artists that should project their shared art even further than that circumstantial stage.

This CD, A Day and a Half, *is the extension of that wonderful instance. Berta Rojas and Paquito D'Rivera meet again in the music of Agustín Pío Barrios and in a selection of popular works. In this way, that "day and a half" turns into an eternity.*

During a great part of his eventful existence, Agustín Pío Barrios Mangoré traveled intensely, taking his wonderful art to large cities and small, lost towns of Latin America. The CD we dedicated to him, *Día y Medio* (A Day and a Half) was nominated for a Latin Grammy in 2012. The Itaú Unibanco sponsored a tour that Berta rightly wanted to call "Por las huellas de Mangoré" ("Following Mangore's Footprints"). This tour has taken us to Chile, Honduras, Puerto Rico, Brazil, the Dominican Republic, Argentina, Uruguay, Guyana, Mexico, and, of course, Paraguay, where the natives had the courtesy of naming me "Beloved Son of Asunción."

The tour plans to have the final concert in El Salvador, featuring the "Chopin of Guitar," as they called the author of the famous "Paraguayan Dance."

Another CD that was nominated in 2013 was *Dances from the New World*, which we had recorded more than five years before with the brothers Odair and Sérgio Assad of the famous duo of Brazilian guitarists, whom I much admired, could finally meet through Yo-Yo Ma, and play with extensively.

One of my early jazz influences in my younger days in Cuba was Carlos Emilio Morales, an extraordinary electric guitarist from whom we learned a lot, especially about bebop harmonies and phrasing. I have applied many of his teachings in this long and tortuous journey, and today, I still steal some of his characteristic phrases, full of wisdom and humor.

On November 12, 2014, with great pain we received the sad news of the passing away of Carlos Emilio, one of my dearest friends as well as a figure very influential on my career. Carlos "El Gordo" (Fats) Emilio (when I met him in the early '60s, he hadn't earned his nickname yet) was one of the most prominent members of the illustrious Cuban guitar tradition, highly respected and admired by colleagues in the jazz, classical, and popular genres of Cuban music.

Born on November 6, 1939, in Marianao, Havana, Carlos Emilio was the son of a dentist. He attended medical school at the University of Havana and worked as a traveling salesman of medical products for several years. But it didn't take long for him to find his true vocation. He learned to play the guitar by himself, with the aid of albums by Latin American trios such as Los Panchos and Los Tres Caballeros. After he discovered jazz, he became an avid record collector. Thanks to him, many of us were first exposed to the work of artists such as Chico Hamilton, Buddy Collette, Barney Kessel, Lee Konitz, Lennie Tristano, Wes Montgomery, Tal Farlow, Ray Brown, Charles Mingus, Oscar Peterson, Horace Silver, and Ornette Coleman. He was soon taking classical guitar lessons and learned sight-reading. These studies enabled him to join the orchestra of the Musial Theatre of Havana, where the prestigious classical guitarist Leo Brouwer worked as a composer. Brouwer was another enthusiastic admirer of El Gordo.

El Gordo's unique style of playing has influenced not only other guitarists, but also many other instrumentalists of various generations of Cuban musicians. El Gordo was the first to suggest to Cuban bassists that they could apply guitar techniques to the Fender bass with great results, instead of trying to play the instrument like a contrabass. Carlitos del Puerto learned this technique directly from El Gordo and later introduced it to a whole new generation of electric bassists on the island. It's amazing that such a timid and humble man could have such a tremendous impact on our lives as instrumentalists.

Throughout my career, I've had the joy of sharing the stage and the recording studio with the greatest guitarists of the most diverse musical genres, from Bucky Pizzarelli and Romero Lubambo to Cubans René Toledo and Flores Chaviano, Israeli Yotam Silberstein and the Brasil Guitar Duo. The last two young men are extraordinary classical guitarists, and like the Assads they have a solid rhythmical and harmonious sense so common among the nationals of the South American giant but frequently rare among so-called classical guitarists.

One of the most versatile among all of the guitarists I've played with is Fareed Haque. It was through him in the 1980s that I got reacquainted with Latin American and Spanish guitar that I listened to when the students played at the Marianao Conservatory. I also recorded several of Lauro's beautiful Venezuelan waltzes. Fareed, whose mother is Chilean and father Pakistani, plays a concert of classical guitar with great ease in the afternoon and that same evening goes to a Chicago club to play blues or to the Kennedy Center in Washington to play Latin jazz, or even organizes jam sessions playing standards, as I've seen him do often. Fareed is formidable!

His Majesty, the Piano

My father used to say that the piano is the king of the instruments. He pointed with reverence at the old, humble upright piano we had in the hallway of our home in Marianao. Our home was in the outskirts of the once-impressive city of La Habana, very close to the legendary Tropicana Club, "The most beautiful cabaret in the world." Ironically, although we befriended so many great pianists, neither my dad nor I ever managed to master the beautiful instrument of Tatum and Chopin. Nevertheless, from a very early age, I have always been blessed to work with great pianists, from Fernando Mulens, Emiliano Salvador, Alon Yavnai, Bebo and Chucho Valdés to even McCoy Tyner, Monty Alexander, Dave Brubeck, Michel Camilo, and others, whose names would fill pages in these brief notes.

A music student once asked Miles Davis, what he could do to be a better trumpet player. Miles, who wasn't a man of words, said, "Buy a piano!" And even if it sounds like a joke or an exaggeration, truth is that knowledge of the keyboard automatically opens a wide horizon of possibilities in harmonic and counterpoint knowledge. The only thing I reproach my father for in my musical education is not sitting me down at the piano instead of giving me this "bumpy whistle" that sounds just one note at a time.

Although the piano is not for everyone, when I was around twelve or thirteen, in the same Caturla Conservatory of Marianao where I studied clarinet with Maestro Enrique Pardo and harmony with Félix Guerrero, I asked a young and already recognized teacher, Ninowska Fernández Brito, to teach me the instrument.

Although I was already ahead in theory, solfege, clarinet, and other subjects, the more I forced myself I could never pass over the second page of the elementary piano book. It seemed that the monody form I had been used to since I was five years old, when I blew my soprano saxophone for the first time, limited my capacity to read two pentagrams at the same time.

Pianists, I mean good ones, harmonically speaking are a bit like poets. They see farther than what the rest of we mortals can see. What normal people see as a pair of chirping birds on an electrical cable poets would describe as "a discreet advance of spring announced by the sweet voices of small feathery angels!" In contrast to those of us that play monody instruments, pianists can think and read lineal and horizontal music simultaneously.

In some piano parts there are melodies and even harmonies for other instruments of the orchestra, so they always know what we are doing, and can play their parts and ours too. If not, they sing it while they accompany. To me, that's like being an "octopus-man," too complicated. We have enough with the reeds and mouthpieces and all that stuff, no? And that's why, Yeyo, I envy pianists. Plus they learn how to play the organ, like that Japanese giant Makoto Ozone, then they have two more notes in their feet!

That Makoto is extraordinary. I met him in New York in 1986, when he played (as he still does) with Gary Burton. Since then, every time I go to Japan I call him to make music. In addition to being a good musician he is a formidable guy; it's very pleasant to hang out with him and his wife Misusu.

In October 2013, Makoto invited me to do a couple of concerts with the Tokyo Metropolitan Symphony, where I played the emblematic Clarinet Concerto in A Major by Mozart and he played Sergei Rachmaninov's wonderful "Rhapsody on a Theme of Paganini." In the second part of the full house program entitled "Jazz Meets the Classics" they took the orchestra out and Makoto and I stayed by ourselves improvising on Chopin, Lecuona, and Bach's music.

That beautiful Mozart concerto for clarinet has been played and recorded by many people. Among them, fabulous clarinetists like Sabine Mayer and Ricardo Morales, who also play it with the basset clarinet, for which the piece was originally written. It's hard (if not useless) to compete with that, so I decided to do the first original movement and the second Adagio movement in the form of blues like I used to play it with Irakere. In the third one Makoto added an improvised section on the original music score of the orchestra, something innovative and unrepeatable. The audience applauded like mad at this, which is not very common in the discreet and moderate Japanese character. This sort of adventure can only take place if you have the versatile and extraordinary hand of a pianist like Makoto Ozone. It has to be someone that knows the so-called classical music and at the same time feels comfortable improvising in several musical styles.

To be able to work with all kinds of pianists is a true bless-ing; you learn something from all of them, watching them play and seeing how they solve the problems that come up in our profession.

Another great and purely classical pianist and educator with whom I had the pleasure to work with was Argentine Aldo Antognazzi, a specialist and a sort of musical biographer of the works of Muzio Clementi, a Roman composer born in 1752 that spent most of his life in England. Mainly known for his beautiful sonatinas, which are a must for all piano students, Clementi was also a pedagogue, orchestra conduc-tor, editor, and manufacturer of keyboard instruments. Few remember Clementi, and he is not often mentioned outside of conservatories, but Aldo rescued him from oblivion by re-cording eleven volumes of all his works. I met Maestro An-tognazzi through his son-in-law, the Argentine saxophonist Oscar Feldman, a New York City resident, married to Aldo's daughter Sandra, an exquisite ballerina. One day, we decided to do a recital tour through many Argentine cities and record the CD *Music from Two Worlds* in Buenos Aires with pieces from Villa-Lobos, Carlos Guastavino, and Brahms, a couple of my pieces, and "The Shepherd on the Rock," the charm-ing piece for clarinet, piano, and soprano voice by Franz Schubert. My wife Brenda Feliciano sang the vocals, and we received a Grammy nomination in 1999.

One of the most original pianists I've ever met was the immense Ignacio Villa, known to all as "Bola de Nieve," or "Snow Ball." Although it's said his style was greatly influenced by Maria Cervantes, Ignacio Cervantes's daughter, who was a singer and pianist, the truth is that Bola was a unique and sensational artist. Ignacio Cervantes was known as the "father of Cuban *pianismo*." His personality was a strange mixture of "Cuban" and universal artist; he sang in English, French, Italian, Catalán, and Portuguese, and he was an artist for all audiences. He had a hilarious kind of sympathy. His style accompanying himself with his piano was passionate, rhythmic, and exquisite.

I suppose, Yeyo, that you know many of these details already, but as this epistle will be published my intention is for the readers to know the life and works of these artists of the past who contributed so much to art and to our lives in general.

Those that knew Bola once he was famous don't know that he started as a silent film pianist, accompanying many singers during the '30s in Havana. He used to go to Mexico frequently because the musical scene there was very important. He traveled with Ernesto Lecuona throughout South America. He accompanied Rita Montaner, who was always a teaser and practical joker. They say she was the first one that called him by his nickname, which he hated, during a performance in Mexico City.

"Rita did me the biggest favor when she named me Bola de Nieve in front of the audience," said the pianist and singer once, "although she did it to bother me."

He was born on September 11, 1911, in Guanabacoa. I don't know if it was Pablo Neruda, Andrés Segovia, or Jacinto Benavente who said, "When Bola sang, nothing further could be done for a song." He had a sharp and hoarse tone of voice. When asked, he said he had the voice of a mango vendor.

Bola was a great cook, and he made the best dark rice with the beans "hidden" (*moros y cristianos*). Around 1985, comedian Guillermo Alvarez Guedes and his wife Elsie invited me to dine at their home in Miami and have "dark rice à la Bola de Nieve." Apparently, he first ground the beans so that when he mixed them with the rice, he stained it without the actual beans. I tried it once. I went with trumpet player Jorge Varona to Bola's apartment on Twenty-Sixth Street above Barbaram's Club, across from the zoo. Something funny happened there, and we learned something new. It was wintertime, which in the Caribbean is very mild, although it was a particularly cold and humid night. We heard a very sharp whistle from outside.

"It's very cold and the monkey whistles," said Bola, who lived across from the zoo.

The conclusion is that precisely on that evening I learned that the old saying "the monkey whistles" is actually true. When monkeys are cold, they shiver and make a sharp sound that could be mistaken for whistling. Years later, when we were living in New York, my mother would tell me whenever it snowed, "Wear warm clothes, son. Tonight the monkey will whistle." It inevitably reminded me of that evening of dark rice and whistling monkeys at the apartment of the great Bola de Nieve.

Once during a European tour, I went with Dizzy Gillespie to visit Bebo Valdés at the beautiful restaurant in Stockholm where he worked the piano bar. Since those days I had the idea of finding a way to record with the "Caballón" (Big Horse), and at the end of the set I asked him if he thought about getting an orchestra together again. He answered that he already had a ten-member orchestra and showed me those two hands with fine long fingers...

"They're never late," he said, "they don't smoke or drink, don't fight with me or amongst themselves, they don't get into drugs or skirt troubles, they don't gossip or chit-chat during rehearsal, they are always happy and ready to work without charging me a penny. The best orchestra in the world, brother!"

Nevertheless, Yeyito, Chucho, Bebo's son recommends that his piano students have a drum, a bongo, a pair of "claves," or any other percussion instrument. Oscar Stagnaro, the Peruvian bassist also recommends this practice, as it gives you a sense of rhythm that will be very useful for understanding whatever the percussionists are cooking. After all, the piano is just another percussion instrument with the advantage of making melodies and harmony, no? So, let's do something, Yeyíssimo. Buy the piano we talked about and next to it place a pair of maracas and a conga drum, and you can split your time between the instruments.

Bebo de Cuba

I don't know if you ever met him, saw him on TV, or heard any of his many records, Yeyito, but I tell you that Bebo Valdés was an artist much in demand during the dynamic and lively musical life in Havana BC (before Castro), not only for his extraordinary charisma and friendliness, but also for his versatility and knowledge of the musical profession.

I've known Bebo since I was a child, although I can't even remember when I saw him for the first time. It could have been at home in Marianao, or at Tropicana, or eating soup at the popular cafeteria "Los Parados" on the corner of Neptuno and Consulado streets in Havana. All the musicians went there around the clock. Perhaps I met him in the small office of musical imports my dad had a few blocks away. The only thing I can say is that he was a truly special man. It's very hard to describe with words someone whom they called "El Caballón" (Big Horse) out of affection and respect in the musical environment of the City of Columns. I suppose they called him that because of his elevated physical and professional stature.

Whenever we would bump into each other, many years later, Bebo liked to speak about his friend Tito, my dad—of their endearing friendship, of the time they both dated two sisters in I don't know what Havana neighborhood, of my dad's grouchiness in those youthful days, and of Tito's devilish double staccato on the tenor saxophone.

"With a pen handy, Bebo was quick and right on the dot," remembered his friend, comedian and record producer Guillermo Alvarez Guedes. "He wrote at daybreak, when he came home to Santa Amalia from his nightclub gig. The following morning at Radio Progreso or at the Panart studio, the arrangement was already copied and ready to record. And it sounded glorious!"

You could hear him just as well at the Hotel Plaza casino conducting his jazz trio with Orestes Urfé on bass and the legendary Guillermo Barreto on the drums, playing the piano in Armando Romeu's orchestra at Tropicana, or recording in a studio with Benny Moré, Celia Cruz, or Nat King Cole, to include even a couple of Norman Granz's productions.

The last image I have of Bebo in Cuba was on a TV show conducting his Sabor de Cuba Orchestra, elegantly dressed in a gray silk tuxedo with black satin flaps. At one corner of the orchestra, to the left of the conductor and sitting on the piano, was a tall, thin young black guy with a long face and thin moustache. It was his son Chucho, who would later on become one of my closest friends and collaborators as well as one of the most positive influences on my career. That was in 1960, when I was twelve or thirteen years of age. I didn't see Bebo again until the summer of 1978, from the stage at Carnegie Hall where Irakere was performing as part of the Newport Jazz Festival. Bebo was, coincidentally, visiting his sister in New York. He had bought a box seat, where he had invited my mother and father, good friends from his youth. I don't have to tell you, dear Yeyito, how things work in the land of rumba. The Cuban authorities vetoed our presence, Bebo told me later that it had been eighteen years since father and son had last communicated with each other. At that time, they were only able to exchange a couple of words far from there. It's a sad story, Yeyo, and it's not worth discussing it now. We better go on with the music, because it's far above all of that.

Much after that sweet-and-sour experience, in 1997, writer Guillermo Cabrera Infante went to Madrid to receive his Cervantes Award from King Don Juan Carlos de Borbón. To celebrate the occasion, Javier Estrella, the event producer, organized a recital in the small, cozy Círculo de Bellas Artes Theater. He recently wrote about it:

> From the beginning, I knew that the best possible concert we could dedicate to Cabrera Infante was to call his dear good friends, Bebo and Paquito, to take him for a ride with their music, through his beloved Havana, the same one where the three of them had left some sad tigers.

Estrella was right. I still think of that memorable evening with my favorite heroes, Cabrera and El Caballón, with nostalgia.

We arrived from Stockholm and New York respectively on the prior afternoon and Bebo's luggage had taken a detour to I don't know what planet, leaving him with only what he was wearing. Luckily, the pianist was always prepared for any unexpected event, and he was, as always, impeccably dressed, with his inseparable navy blue blazer and tie. More than a Caribbean pianist, he looked like an Italian aristocrat who had stayed too long in the sun.

Around eight or nine p.m. we went to the beautiful apartment facing Parque del Retiro, where my good friend Carlos Alberto Montaner and his charming wife Linda had invited us to dinner with Patricia and Alvaro, the son of Mario Vargas Llosa, and his wife. The Montaners often have illustrious guests, and although the dinner was delicious and the conversation stimulating, the one who stole the show that evening was Linda and Carlos's granddaughter. With a mixture of ingenuity and overwhelming logic typical of children, the little girl asked her grandfather if Mr. Bebo was an African king.

We all laughed, and probably no one remembers the writer's answer today, but El Caballón (no wonder they gave him that nickname) really had an impressive, majestic presence, upright on his six-foot-plus height. That's why the little girl wasn't far from the truth when she thought she saw a symbol of nobility in the musician's slim figure.

Looking back today, when the great pianist from Quivicán is no longer with us, I see that among so many valuable things I inherited from my father was the tender friendship with this immense body and soul of a man, a true king of hearts, wise, affectionate, mythical, and very simple at the same time. I can also say with true pride that one of the happiest and on-target moments of my career was when in 1994 I convinced the German company Messidor to produce the CD *Bebo Rides Again*, after El Caballón had been away from a recording studio for more than three decades.

Undoubtedly, Bebo Valdés was, artistically and humanly, a unique personality that epitomizes the Cuban musician's elegance in an era unfortunately lost in time and space, completely incompatible with the vulgar epidemic that has infested the profession in our impoverished island for more than fifty long years.

The Piano and the Thousand Cans of Milk

Virgilio Vixama "El Jamaiquino" (The Jamaican), an old, black, wise man who played baritone saxophone with Benny Moré's famous "Tribe," lamented in earnest, "I always like to get paid for my gigs in advance, because when the music is gone with the wind and the party's over, everybody splits the joint and forgets to pay the musicians."

The Jamaican was a sui-generis kind of cat who wore very long jackets, suspenders, and loose pants in the style of the "Barbarian of Rhythm," as they called Benny Moré. Tall, hefty, and with very dark skin, he inherited his nickname from his father, who was of Haitian and not Jamaican descent, and who earned his living in another era, buying and selling musical instruments and whatever other crapola he came across.

For some reason that, like I said before, I cannot fathom everybody in our country calls all Spaniards Galician, the Asians are all lumped in the category of Chinese, and all the Jews are Poles. So Virgilio's father, who was born in Haiti, was "The Jamaican." There's no figuring out these crazy Cubans!

As Generoso Jiménez told me, the son looked very much like the father, they both had the same deer-caught-inheadlights expression and those restless bug eyes. He had worked and traveled with our character throughout the island and Latin America, playing with Benny's big band.

Another eccentricity: Virgilio Vixama was the only person I had ever seen who could move, simultaneously and in different directions, his right eye, his left eye, and the cigar that was always dangling, halfway lit, from his mouth.

He gestured wildly as he engaged in lively conversations about various subjects, patting the beads of perspiration on his ebony face without ever letting his impeccable white hankie even brush the ashen end of his cigar. And it was quite a show to watch him rotate that cigar from one side of his mouth to the other as words spewed uninterruptedly from those sides free of the thick tobacco stick.

Referring to the Jamaican, "Tojo" Jiménez once said to me, "If truth be told, Virgilio wasn't very good at reading music on first sight, but street smart as he was, if he spotted too many notes in any one passage, he clung to the first and last ones. By doing that he avoided many a tight spot. Once he had learned the piece, he played it with a lot of swing. He escaped from Tamakún, that Jamaican dude!"

"Tamakún?" I asked.

"Yeah, Tamakún, the errant avenger," said Tojo. "He was the leading character of a radio soap with Jesús Alvariño, who was very famous on Cuban radio during the nineteen-forties and nineteen-fifties."

Then, the walking encyclopedia called Cristóbal Díaz-Ayala to clarify over the telephone from San Juan, Puerto Rico, and it turned out the entire phrase was "He escaped right from under Tamakún's turban!" Cuban jive, bro!

Pucho Escalante, the trombone player from Guantanamo who lived in Caracas for many years, used to tell me that Benny Moré was very popular among Venezuelans, which is why he always played the carnival seasons there.

After he finished his work, Pucho remembered with a smile, Virgilio Vixama would spread open a blanket on the sidewalks of Caracas and sell the clothes that he'd brought in his suitcase from Cuba. Sometimes he even sold the blanket! Then he'd just board the plane with whatever he was wearing and went home with his baritone sax and the little extra money he made inside the huge pockets of his orchestra uniform. Too damn much, that Jamaican.

My father had a modest little import shop, where he sold musical instruments, accessories, and books; it was on the second floor of Virtues #57, between Prado and Consulado. Every day, such people walked in as Cachao, Ernesto Lecuona, Fernando Mulens, author and sax player Leonardo Acosta, Mario Bauzá, Bebo Valdés, Pedrito Knight, and Chico O'Farrill. The Jamaican was also a frequent visitor at the store owned by Tito, my dad, to buy reeds, for instance, and other musical accessories. During the time when I first met him, I was a child, you could still (unfortunately) smoke everywhere, so I don't remember ever seeing Virgilio Vixama without a huge cigar in his mouth and a gas lighter in his right hand, always set to ready, aim, and fire.

At the end of the day, Tito liked to get together with his friends from that wonderful music world of Havana, at the Los Parados cafeteria, right on the corner of Consulado and Neptuno, a block and a half from his office. I remember that among those present that afternoon were singer Miguelito

Valdés, "Chocolate" Armenteros, the trumpet player, and Richard Egües, the flutist from the Orquesta Aragón. Virgilio was advising a young musician who'd recently come to the capital from the countryside how to survive in Havanaland (as he called the capital).

"To survive in Havanaland you have to do everything I do. I blow five different whistles, bro—alto, tenor, baritone, and the dangerous 'licorice stick' that I more or less manage to scratch." (He meant the clarinet.)

Virgilio had lived in Mexico for a few years during the 1940s. In the land of the Aztecs he married a white and very petite Mexican woman. She had a gentle and demure way about her that made for a sharp contrast with the tall stature, dark skin, and explosive, expansive nature of the man she loved with quiet devotion. He had two children with her, both born in Mexico: Villito, who turned out white but looked exactly like him, with his naive smile and his pushed down nose, and the little one, Victor, who had darker skin but in turn looked a lot more like his white Mexican mother.

Warm, friendly and outgoing, with his raspy and potent voice, Virgilio the Jamaican said the funniest things when you least expected. Sometimes telling a joke was the furthest thing from his mind, and when everyone burst out laughing, he was the first one to be surprised.

"Damn it, *cuate*. A person can't even talk seriously anymore here," he'd exclaim with his Cuban accent sprinkled with Mexican expressions. This would just provoke even more laughter among the group of friends that surrounded him.

Victim of a galloping cirrhosis of the liver that ended his life on February 19, 1963, the golden voice of Benny Moré, that most popular of Cuban artists, sang no more. His multitudinous funeral service in Havana was only comparable to that of his compatriot, Celia Cruz, four decades later in "the city that never sleeps."

Around that time, Alfonso Arau, a versatile Mexican comic, fell in love with the Revolution and decided to part ways with his partner, Sergio Corona, to remain in Cuba. Arau was in the process of preparing a theater project, and, with funding from the Cuban government, he founded the Gran Teatro de la Habana, remodeling the Alcázar Theatre, or the former Theatre Alhambra, on Consulado Street and the corner of Virtudes, right in the very heart of the City of Columns. While the site was still under construction, Arau rehearsed his new experimental group of actors-dancers-singers and orchestra in what was once the ancient Convent of Santa Clara in Old Havana, confiscated by the government from the Catholic monks.

After the death of Benny Moré, Virgilio bounced around from one job to the next until Tony Taño, conductor of the orchestra of the Gran Teatro, invited him to join in. And it was in that theater, next to such illustrious colleagues as Chucho Valdés, Alfonso Arau, Bobby Carcassés, Carlos Emilio Morales, and Leo Brouwer, that Virgilio Vixama blew his "five whistles" in Cuba for the last time. I also played with them and had a lot of laughs with the Jamaican in that Convent of Santa Clara and later on in the orchestra pit of the old Alcázar, when at last the doors of the spanking new Gran Teatro de la Habana opened to the public, with a play by Segundo Cazalis entitled *Oh, La Gente!*

The government closed down my father's little import shop, and he started to work in Teatro Martí with the Rodrigo

Prats Orchestra. The last batch of Selmer musical instruments had arrived in 1961, aboard the French ship *Le Coubre*. Just moments after the instruments and cargo was unloaded, the ship blew up violently, sinking with a huge other shipment of explosives and firearms that the French government had sold to Fidel Castro. One curious fact was that it was on that occasion that the lens of photographer Alberto Korda captured the historic image of Che Guevara seen around the world on T-shirts, watches, baseball caps, and any other piece of capitalist consumerism imaginable.

After confiscating every private enterprise on the island, the Cuban government began to import musical instruments from the Soviet bloc, but those pieces of junk were useless to Cuban musicians. To this day, just like with those phenomenal American cars that have circulated the streets of Havana for more than fifty years, the instruments that my father Tito imported are the ones that are still played in Cuban orchestras.

No sooner had I began my joyous season at the Gran Teatro de la Habana, I was inducted into mandatory military service. Segundo Cazalis sailed for Venezuela where he would die years later, and Arau grew tired of making tourism with foreign revolutions and took his music to Hollywood by way of Mexico. One of his sons, composer Eduardo Gamboa, was born in Cuba during those days of arduous daily rehearsals at the Convent of Santa Clara. As an adult, "Eduardito the Cuban," as his older half-brother Fernando Arau Corona called him, took the last name of his mother, Mexican actress Emily Gamboa, separating himself once and for all from the last name of his famous father. Fernando, for his part, is the son from his father's first marriage, to the sister of his former partner Sergio Corona, and rumor has it that the exceptional duo of comic dancers dissolved along with the Arau-Corona marriage. Juicy gossip, eh?

In those days (not to say from the very first day) obtaining provisions was becoming a hairy proposition in Cuba, and what they gave out, according to the ration book, could fit into Mother Goose's thimble. Virgilio, with a Mexican wife and two children to support spent his days, as he used to say, hustling on one foot in the suffocating and oppressive heat of the Havana streets. Wearing a pair of pants that he'd cut off at the knees, very worn-out slippers, an old and frayed pajama top, and with an empty sack of sugar on his back, "El Jamaiquino" shuffled throughout the city searching for malanga (a tuber that is good for the little ones' stomachs), beans, rice, and especially milk on the black market for his kids. I mention dairy products in particular because it is still hard to believe that, in Cuba, the daily liter of milk they ration to each child is taken away when they turn seven. Between seven and eleven years of age, each child is given only one liter of yogurt, and for each adult, three cans of condensed or evaporated milk *a month*! And that was before we all donated, "voluntarily," one can from each quota to send to the Chilean brothers. The same happened to the pound of sugar we had to send the Peruvians God knows when. Not to mention when General Augusto Pinochet sent Salvador Allende and his cronies to a better world; Velasco Alvarado blew up like the *USS Maine*, and the can of milk and the pound of sugar never returned to the quota of the common man.

"Maaan," said the clever musician. "And remember what Che Guevara told us one time at the CTC, that in a couple of years Cuba would produce more milk than Holland?" Breaking a sweat, rotating his eyes and his cigar (also contraband) from one side of his mouth to the other, he continued. "I trade shaving razors for cigars, people," he offered to passersby.

Most likely pressured by his wife and by the untenable family situation, Virgilio ran out of verses to sing to his very Mexican *Aeneid*. Abiding by the nationality of his wife and children, he asked for permission to leave the island. That started the downward spiral, since, just as everyone else who asks to leave the country is let go from his place of work, Vixama was fired from his job at the Gran Teatro. Then things got even harder for him. Whenever people saw him with his burlap sack, hustling for the family's daily bread, nobody knew where he got the money to pay for what he bought on the black market.

One day a rumor began to circulate that the authorities had caught Virgilio with a thousand cans of condensed milk and arrested him. "No way a thousand cans of milk would fit into his old and frayed burlap sack," I thought. Then people were saying that the police found the thousand cans hidden inside his house, or behind a piano. But I remembered that the only keyboard the Jamaican had was a tiny Spinet in the living room of his apartment, and even if he had had Liberace's piano, he wouldn't have been able to stash away so many cans of milk.

Then they changed the story to Virgilio getting caught selling a thousand cans of milk or running around with a stack of bills in his pocket looking for someone who would sell him a thousand cans of milk, that the President of the CDR or Neighborhood Committee had snitched on him and he was taken to the police station. The guard on duty that day knew him from back in the days of the dance parties with Benny Moré, and after listening to the accusations against the musician, he said, "Please gentlemen, let this man go immediately. Don't you realize there aren't one thousand cans of milk in all of Havana, not even in the official warehouse of the Ministry of Commerce?"

I don't know, but it was apparent that Virgilio Vixama never lost his sense of humor, not even during the most harrowing moments. In the middle of that tragic farce, I remember thinking to myself, such misfortune and terrible timing—after they had waited so long, the departure date for him and his family was, as they say, just around the corner.

Finally, in 1973, we found out that Virgilio was officially allowed to travel to Mexico to reunite with his family, who'd managed to leave the island some months before. What I didn't find out until much later was that Villito, his oldest son, had to stay behind in Cuba for almost eight more years, since Immigration denied his exit permit.

It was close to the ill-fated days of the 11,000 refugees inside the Peruvian embassy and the Mariel Exodus, which dumped more than 125,000 Cubans fleeing hunger and oppression on the coasts of Florida. The meetings of repudiation, orchestrated by the government and carried out by street mobs, made life impossible for those who publicly voiced their intention of abandoning the country.

"Leave, dregs of society!" the vulgar throngs chanted in unison. "Leave, anti-social elements!"

The walls of the homes of the ostracized were scribbled with obscenities, and the police simply watched as the enflamed masses threw eggs, rocks, and excrement.

Since Villito had lost touch with the music scene, I tried to phone him, but his number was disconnected. One afternoon, when we had a rehearsal at the terrific hall inside the synagogue that the Ministry of Culture had confiscated from the Jews on Linea Street in the Vedado suburb, I decided to go by the Vixama apartment, which was nearby, to see how things were going with my old friend Virgilio's oldest son. The sun was coming up, and the scarcity of cars in the streets at least made the air purer and more breathable. Sometimes it was difficult to walk on the concrete, raised by the powerful roots of the poplars. The chirping of the sparrows mixed in with the rustling of the giant trees' pointed leaves, filling the quiet with an effervescent and delicious music. But that ineffable sense of peace was intermittently interrupted by the tension created throughout the city by the gangs that terrorized the "ungrateful worms who betrayed the country." The atmosphere became more rarified by the minute, and the situation grew progressively sadder and more uncomfortable.

When I got to the building, a car from the Ministry of the Interior was parked next to the sidewalk, and leaning against a wall by the entrance, a man in uniform, with a semi AKG, yawned to the adagio of the afternoon. Although the armed military are nothing new in the middle of the city in Cuba, I couldn't help but shiver with fear.

"Good afternoon, compañero," I murmured timidly.

Undecided as to whether to go in or move on, I heard the sleepy soldier, without taking his cigarette out of his mouth, muttering something like a grunt of acknowledgment and a military salute. My fears dissipated, and I dared to walk through the small main entrance to the building. An aroma like the soup my grandma used to make, with a lot of cumin, pervaded the hall, and I overheard a woman screaming to a willful child, "Well, you're not setting foot outside until you eat all your soup, do you hear me? Little bastard!"

I went up the scratched granite stairs, and when I reached the floor where the Vixamas lived, I found the door half open. The electricity had come back on, and through the speakers of some radio on the floor above came the caressing and familiar voice of "The Barbarian of Rhythm": *Ooooohhhh Vidaaa, no me dejes.* In my mind's eye I saw the image, not so much of the singer, but of the Jamaican, at the end of the row of saxes in Benny's "Tribe," with his loose and flowing beige suit and shiny Selmer baritone my father Tito had sold him in the little shop on Virtudes Street hanging from his bullish neck. Such memories swept over me with that bolero, so many friends who had left, leaving their baggage in our hearts, as if they would suddenly reappear at any moment.

I knocked on the door, softly at first and then harder. I pushed it open and entered the small living room, which looked as if someone was in the middle of moving. The furniture was piled up, the few ornaments were in boxes or thrown about the place, and against the wall was the piano that had once been the talk of the town among the musicians of Havana. Hanging from a hook by the entrance, exhausted and deflated, was the legendary burlap sack that had so well served the family in hard times.

"Villito! Hey, Villitoooo! You around?"

There was no answer. I caressed the burlap sack like it was an old and defeated animal. I approached the small piano, where there was still a gold and pink frame with a family photograph that showed a happier Virgilio, with his smile and his eternal cigar hanging from his fine black lips, surrounded by his wife and children, one of them still in the arms of his mother. On the wall, another photograph of Benny Moré, wearing a Texan hat, with his cane, dancing in front of his "Tribe." In the orchestra I was able to spot "Chocolate," the trumpet player, Generoso Jiménez, Fernando Álvarez of the silken voice, and, of course, the Jamaican.

"That citizen you are looking for is probably on his flight to Mexico, compañero," said the voice behind me.

I turned around and found myself before a typically dumb sort of Cuban yahoo, with copper skin leathered by the sun and wooden features, one of those they brought down to Havana from the Oriente province to work at the most repressive organisms of the government. The man wore the same uniform as the one who was standing by the entrance, except he was shirtless, with a gun in the holster of his belt, and sweaty. In one hand, he held the case of one of Virgilio's five whistles and in the other, a piece of cardboard about thirty by sixty centimeters long. The carton was scrawled with a thick carpenter's pencil and fastened at two points by a little thin rope, as if ready to be hung from a nail.

"The Revolution has been generous towards that citizen and has allowed him to leave the country to reunite with his family," the soldier said. He placed the case of the instrument next to the other knick-knacks and put the rustic sign carelessly atop the piano stand. Then, without paying too much attention to me, he walked calmly back into the apartment, whistling a Mexican *ranchera*.

When the soldier vanished from my sight into one of the rooms, I got curious and turned to take a look at the piece of cardboard he'd left behind. I couldn't suppress a thunderous laugh when I read the phrase written on it, which looked like a product of the mind of a Cuban-born Franz Kafka: "TRADING A PIANO FOR A THOUSAND CANS OF MILK."

"Oh, Virgilio, Virgilio, there will never be anyone like you!" I shouted out loud, as if he could still hear me. I heard the echo of the wooden man's laughter all the way from the back room.

Havana, Enchanted Paradise

My Havana sleeps
The silence watches over the dawn in shadows
A streetlight licks the asphalt with its luminous tongue
We hear the tired key of a good little rumba
The last one of the night
—Alvaro de Villa

Pucho Escalante, or "Big Head Pucho," as his friends affectionately called him (and God knows he had friends coming out of the woodwork), was filled with enthusiasm and contagious joy. He played the trombone and was a popular character in Havana's music scene and practical joker. Rumor has it that back in the day, he and actor Guillermo Alvarez Guedes got the local circus midget really drunk. They shaved his moustache, got him stark naked, put a diaper on him, and left him in front of Havana's national orphanage, La Casa de Beneficencia. According to his blessed Aunt Adelfa, this act was a huge sacrilege that in 1950s Havana could be punished by excommunication from the church.

Escalante was also seen inside the running convertible of saxophonist Lito Rivas when they threw rotten fruits and eggs at the Navy Band's bassist. The unfortunate marine named Peña was dressed in his impeccably white uniform waiting for his date at the corner of the Payret Theater, across from the Capitol Building and the Galician Center. The poor man ran and ran behind the car using his arms to dodge the foul-smelling rotten fruit pouring over him. The cruel attack ended when Lito noticed in the rearview mirror that the distressed marine remembered his regulation Colt .38 revolver and was pulling it out of its cartridge belt. He stepped on the gas pedal and turned at full speed at the northwest corner of Central Park towards the Manzana de Gómez. They had already lost sight of the marine when they heard two shots. A cloud of pigeons and sparrows was lifted in midst of the chaos-packed park. Dogs barked, and people ran in all directions. A frightened Pucho threw himself out of the car and walked until he disappeared into the streets of old Havana. He got lost, and no one knew where to find him.

"I have no clue as to where Pucho is hiding, but until that rascal turns up, I have tickets to see the ballet performance at the Auditorium Theater. How do you like that?" said Chalo, the fugitive trombonist's brother.

That afternoon's program at the beautiful Calzada Street theater featured *Petrushka*, with Igor Stravinsky's music. The phenomenal Fokine choreography was by Alberto Alonso as the soloist, with the flawless musical interpretation directed by Catalonian musician José Ardévol. We left the theater in total awe.

"Hey, Chalito, where have you been, honey?" said an almost six-foot-tall pretty blonde gringa. She stamped a kiss on his lips, and even I felt its wetness; it was as torrid as an earthquake.

"You promised to take me dancing with the Márquez Sisters at the outdoor cafés, remember?"

Then, pointing at me she added, "We can always take your friend with us to escort Fefita. She'll be here any minute. What do you say, guys?"

I interrupted. "I'm sorry, Chalo, but please tell Ginger Rogers here that my English didn't pass the second lesson, so with anything other than 'Tom is a boy and Mary is a girl,' I am as lost as a cockroach in a chicken party. Okay?" I thought what I said came out pretty smoothly.

She was watching us. My English must have sounded to her like Chinese or Martian. The American lady might not have understood a word I said, but she and Chalo couldn't stop laughing. When they finally stopped, Chalo said not to worry, that the blonde spoke some Spanish and we would wait for her girlfriend to go dancing. We'd go under Prado's awnings, to the outdoor café of the Hotel Pasaje, where the Márquez Sisters and the Anacaona Orchestra were playing.

The Saratoga, The Dorado, and The Pasaje were the three main cafés with live music. These famous outdoor cafés, also known as Las Marquesinas de Prado (the Awnings of Prado), were across from the National Capitol Building, built during Gerardo Machado's dictatorship. These places all featured women's orchestras like Renovación, Anacaona, Las Cubanitas, and Ensueño. They were as good as, and sometimes even better, than those of the opposite sex. The main course was undoubtedly the dynamic Marquez Sisters, whose performance was not to be missed.

The night was still young and beautiful, so, as soon as Fefita, Ginger Rogers's girlfriend (and what a girlfriend!) came from the "pipi-room," we were off. From that night on, Chalo's blondie became Ginger Rogers for everybody. After the show, we took a walk under Prado's laurel grove heading to Avenida de los Presidentes. We passed the hotel by the same name, near the gigantic statue of Don Tomás Estrada Palma, the first president of Cuba. We continued down the street near the modern American embassy building and stopped around the monument to the armored ship *Maine*, whose explosion started the Spanish-American War. Behind it, the formidable Hotel Nacional stood majestic on its rocky promontory.

We sat on the Malecón's thick contention wall to enjoy the soft breeze. The croak of marine birds got me out of my contemplative ecstasy that until then had kept me from looking anywhere but at Fefita's cleavage. She was a national beauty. She contemplated the moon's reflection on the quiet waters of the Florida Strait. Fefita was one of those gorgeous Cuban ladies you could get rich selling tickets for people just to watch. She was a demolition crew, a hurricane, and as bubbly as Alka-Seltzer. With her big black eyes, her meaty lips like the pulp of a ripe *caimito* (Luis Carbonell would call it *cuasi bemba*), and a behind of metaphysical dimensions. It balanced harmoniously with the rhythm of the ascending walk she had polished to perfection. Anyone who crossed her path would succumb to her beauty. Although she was named like the danzón she could have very well been the one and only *Trigueña Encarnación*, the unbelievable brunette in Orquesta Aragón's popular song featuring Richard Egües's flute.

When we were ready to start to walk back to Las Marquesinas, a persistent blowing horn and a loud male voice yelling and waving his arms at us like a windmill made us come to a stop. Lito Rivas, in his green Ford convertible, created such a commotion that it almost interfered with the traffic. He was inviting us for a ride through Malecón in his famous convertible.

Through the speakers we could hear the beautiful ode to Havana by Costa Rican composer Ray Tico: "Havana, enchanted paradise/Havana, princess of the seas."

A few minutes later we passed by General Antonio Maceo's monument. The tall pedestal seemed to raise the statue of our Bronze Titan right into the sky, as if he was riding his white horse among the stars. A magical and mysterious aura surrounded that ancient building that housed "La Casa de Beneficiencia" and the city with heavy upright yellowish walls. This city has been a source of inspiration for poets, musicians, writers, and landscape artists for more than four centuries.

As Dominican writer Juan Bosch writes in his book, *Cuba, the Fascinating Island*,

> *It didn't take long for Havana to turn into a center of great commercial and cultural activities. It was born, nonetheless, by itself, without a royal disposition, or formal document to give her a name. Historians can't even come to terms with where it was first established. For a long time they argued whether it was called Havana, Abana, Avanam, or Habana. What we do know for sure is that between 1515 and 1529, small shacks and settlements began to appear in the bay's eastern shore. The surrounding land belonged, or was ruled by "Cacique Habaguanex," and from him came the name of what in time would become the capital of the Pearl of the Antilles and the gate to the Indies.*

In its most glorious days, Havana came to be a sort of synthesis between the immense New York nightlife and the relaxed bohemian frivolity of Paris, but without the harshness of the northern winter and with that omnipresent, all-enveloping smell of the sea instead of the implacable, always-stalking European body odor so common in the City of Light and all over the old continent. On the other hand, there were those who saw the impudent Cuban capital as a Caribbean version of Sodom and Gomorrah, whose many aberrant perversions required a titanic effort to avoid.

Legend has it that when Bishop Fray Diego de Compostela arrived in Havana on November 17, 1687, he learned that a newborn baby, abandoned on the city streets, had been eaten by pigs. So affected was the clergyman that he had the happy idea of opening a home for all the helpless children. He died in 1704 and couldn't see his idea through, but the plan was carried out, inaugurated on the corner of Oficios and Muralla streets around 1710 by his successor, the illustrious Bishop Jerónimo Valdés. It was situated in several homes known throughout the years as Casa Cuna (literally "Crib Home") and later as Maternity. The charity house was moved to the place it occupied for many years on the corner of San Lázaro and Belascoaín, sponsored by the Countess of Jaruco, the Marquess of Arcos y de Cárdenas, and the canon Luis Peñalever in 1792.

It seemed to one walking around the silent hallways, basements, and tunnels of the very ancient construction as if the thick walls hid thousands of stories that had been floating for centuries in the humid, cold echo. One of the best known ones was the one about the boy that was deposited there in 1809 and became, years later, the distinguished poet Gabriel de la Concepción Valdés, or Plácido, who shone with his own light as a man of words until the despotic colonial government cut off his life, involving him in what history knew as "La Conspiración de la Escalera" (The Conspiracy of the Ladder). It was found later that Plácido had been born in Matanzas as a result of an illicit love affair between a mixed-race hairdresser and a dancer from Burgos that had come to work at Havana's Teatro Principal.

Another celebrated character on the orphanage books was Cecilia Valdés, immortalized by Cirilo Villaverde in his passionate novel *La Loma del angel (Angel Hill)*. With a script by Austin Rodríguez, the drama of Cecilia Valdés was taken to the stage by Maestro Gonzalo Roig's zarzuela, becoming the most representative work of Cuban lyric art. Even with fictitious names it seemed to have actually happened; several historians later verified facts, addresses, and costumes given by the novelist.

Galician Benigno, who was a sort of orphanage concierge for many years, insisted that on the nights of full moon, the voice of Plácido could be heard reciting his poems. And he said he had seen with his own eyes the ghost of Cecilia, who, still weeping over Leonardo's betrayal, dragged her sorrowful soul in between the columns of the orphanage. Certainly, the basement and subterranean hallways could give you chills, but that somber and dreadful environment changed the moment you stepped onto the huge central patio under the golden sun shining in Havana's blue sky.

It is unbelievable that the most beautiful song composed about Havana was not written by a native or a Cuban, but by a

Costa Rican, Ray Tico, who, like many others, fell in love with the fabulous city.

Upon turning right, near Castillo de La Punta, we immediately bumped into the two bronze lions that guard Paseo del Prado. We followed the beautiful avenue toward the outdoor cafes. The exhilarating aroma emanating from the pores of the storybook female by my side was driving me nuts. Her wild jet-black hair brushing my face and the wind whispering to the blackbirds on top of the trees blended with the melody and final words of Tico's love song to "Havana, enchanted land of love."

The car seemed to glide softly up the street, leaving behind the Fausto Theater, the Sevilla Biltmore Hotel's Arab Club, and the famous "Engañadora" corner. This spot and "La Engañadora" were both immortalized by composer Enrique Jorrín in his famous "Cha Cha Cha." Restaurant Miami was also right on this corner. We went by the Louvre sidewalk, with Hotel Inglaterra and its souvenir stores bursting with artistically carved maracas, preserved crocodiles, postcards, straw hats with colorful ribbons, and other general tourist trappings. Then, when we crossed San Rafael Street, we saw the National Theater with the Galician Center building, built between 1909 and 1915, right across from Parque Central. This historical ride brought to mind the bomb explosion in the theater's dungeons set by bellicose trade unionists during Enrico Caruso's performance in 1920. Verdi's *Aida* was playing, and Caruso was so frightened, he ran through the streets of Havana dressed as Rhadames.

We crossed San José Street and parked in one of the diagonal squares in the center of the avenue, right between the Capitol building and the café's porches.

As soon as the motor stopped, we could hear the stylish local voices of the Márquez Sisters Trio singing *"Cuidaíto, compay gallo, cuidaíto!"* ("Watch out, cocky buddy, just watch out!"), the delightful guaracha by Ñico Saquito. The place was full to capacity, but we were miraculously able to get the last available table.

"Hello, honey! You did show up!" said a great-looking, trendy mulatta melodiously.

She placed one of her neatly manicured hands on Lito's shoulder. The man stood up, put her hand between his, and after inhaling her fine aroma, kissed her cheek. Then, addressing us, he said, "Guys, this is Graciela, the superstar singer of the Anacaona Orchestra, the one that drives Havana's men wild." Then, pulling a chair and gently inviting the singer to sit with us, he asked, "Isn't that so, Gracielita?"

"Don't elevate me so much, sweetie, or the fall could be shocking, okay?" answered Graciela playfully. Then, in a much lower voice, she added, "And you better watch it, Lito. That sailor is still looking around to break your bones, you hear?"

Looking at his fingernails, Lito said in a clarifying manner, "That little problem is more than taken care of. Peña—that's the name of the bassist you are referring too—loves to fish, and since yesterday was his birthday, which he celebrates along with his mother's, I got together with Alvarez Guedes and bought him the most fabulous fishing gear we found at Sears. Latest model fishing rod, lures, spools, the works. We even got him a hat like those little hats gringos wear in the movies when they go fishing. We also sent his mom the most alluring load of roses, lilies, carnations, and white lilies that we found in the same market where we had bought the rotten fruit. We included a bottle of El Gaitero cider, a note apologizing and promising never to bother him again. Oh, and we also sent a birthday card to Doña Dorita. How about that? Isn't it moving?"

"Yes, very tender," said Nersa Márquez, who had just sat at our table with her sister Trini. Then she added ironically, "So what did you give the midget? A tricycle? Or a box of diapers so the nuns could change him more often? Go ahead, tell us."

Lito replied, "Look, girls, you know that every time someone plays a bad trick on someone, they blame me. But, without accusing anyone, I have to say the midget thing sounds like something Big Head Pucho would do with Trio Taicuba's Cataneo. You know they do that stuff, and when the orphanage gag happened I wasn't even around here, believe it or not." But the practical-joking saxophonist confessed, "I don't deny I would have had fun."

Right at that moment, the music started and we all went to shake our bones to the famous Anacaona rhythms.

"Look at Ginger Rogers and Chalo Astaire dancing like in the movies!" shouted Graciela while heading towards the dance floor.

I was just silently praying that they would play a nice soft bolero so I could slow dance and get closer to Fefita's wet and fragrant neck, which already had me hallucinating. When we got back to the table we were all discussing the new unknown, bizarre-looking member of the Anacaonas.

"I wonder who that weird skinny woman is," exclaimed Trini Márquez.

The skinny clumsy girl with the tambourine face had long and reddish stringy hair. She was wearing sunglasses in the middle of the night, so she looked like a blind woman.

"She looks like a Jamaican hen, you know, the kind with no feathers on their neck," said Nersa, laughing out loud.

Truthfully, the girl didn't exactly look like the models that come out in magazines, but her trombone sounded awesome.

Dos gardenias para ti
Con ellas quiero decir
Te quiero, te adoro

Two gardenias just for you
With them I want to say
I love you, I adore you

It was Graciela's romantic voice, singing (at last) that awaited bolero by Isolina Carrillo, but it was too late for my slow dance. Galleguito Godínez was already bringing the food we ordered, and Fefa was hungry and ready to attack it. The waiter had forgotten to bring the drinks. Glancing all over the place looking for him, we noticed that the weird new trombonist had disappeared from the stage, chair and all. Next, we got the surprise of our lives.

The men's bathroom door opened violently, and a naked man, dressed only in the long, red, messy wig jumped out. It was none other than Pucho Escalante. He ran out the door, jumped over the piano, ran over a waiter, everything on his tray flying all over the place. Pucho bluntly turned several tables full of food and liquor upside down and made his way like a thunderbolt across from us. Then, as if completely suicidal, he crossed the busy street without even looking, forcing cars to slam their screeching breaks and honk their horns like crazy.

"Pucho, hey, Puchooooooo!" Trini, Nersa, Lito, the girls, and I screamed.

Most of all, his brother Chalo called him, but we didn't get his attention. He was gone. We saw him inexplicably reach the other side of the four-lane avenue in one piece. He disappeared from the view around San José Street heading toward the Campoamor Theater. When Pucho got lost in the indistinguishable multitude, we looked back at the bathroom door. Lito and Chalo identified Peña, the Navy bassist, dressed in his white uniform. With him was the circus midget. They were both holding guns and laughing out loud, so hard their jaws were shaking. Later on we learned that they had made the trombonist take off his clothes at gunpoint, making him run stark naked all over the streets of Havana in order to save his life. And what was worse, the weapons were toy guns!

Saxophone vs. Clarinet

On many occasions, I've been asked if I prefer the saxophone to the clarinet, and, Yeyo, truth is, I never know how to answer. It all depends on how I feel when I wake up in the morning. Each instrument has its charm, and deciding which one I prefer is not an option for me. The difference between the two, these cousins with common trunks but such unalike branches, is precisely what is fascinating. As far as the similarities between both, the most notable is the common suffering with the damn reeds; how we clarinetists and saxophonists suffer trying to find a good one that works is indescribable.

It is a mandatory subject in our conversations, how bad the reeds are lately, and I've heard about it for the past sixty years. There are lucky people like Michael Brecker and Ricardo Morales, who have solved the problem using Fibra-Cel, Légère, and others made out of synthetic materials. I used them too for some time (a happy time!), and I even played, I think it was Weber's "Clarinet Concerto No. 2" in Costa Rica with one of them. But in the long run I had to get back to the *Arundo donax*, which is the scientific name of the bamboo-like plant used to make the reeds for all woodwind instruments.

Yet, in spite of this neuralgic detail of the reeds, in my opinion, which is the same for millions of people around the world, the saxophone is one of the most outstanding and useful inventions of the nineteenth century and, actually, of all time.

Adolphe Sax was a controversial man who possessed unlimited creativity and tenacity. A Belgian instrument designer, he created the saxophone around 1841. Adolphe was the son of a well-known manufacturer from whom he learned the trade, an innate inventor who patented many products, including some for the medical industry, and, like many creators, a victim of misunderstanding, envy, and xenophobia from his colleagues, when he moved to France, where the musical industry was much richer than in Belgium. Sax, who had an eventful life, had to declare himself bankrupt several times, and he died in poverty, without ever dreaming of the great impact his innovative artifact would have on the music world.

The young, passionate, and obsessive Belgian inventor had achieved, with his new creation unifying metallic body and clarinet mouthpiece, a volume, tone, and, above all, joyful sound flexibility. No member of the woodwind family had ever before achieved such a sound—not even the saxophone's cousin the clarinet, obscure and melancholic but sometimes kind of hysterical and loud in the sharp notes.

With all its defects, the clarinet is the clarinet, and I'll never forget that it was the recording of a clarinetist, Benny Goodman, that placed in my infantile mind the illusion of becoming a musician in New York, the city of my dreams.

We clarinetists, as a rule, are very gregarious people. Throughout the years, with the sad exception of Benny

Goodman, who passed before I could meet him personally, I've had the opportunity to meet and collaborate with colleagues I have admired, from Eddie Daniels, Buddy DeFranco, and Victor Goines to Mariam Adams of Imani Winds, Paulo Sérgio Santos, Anat Cohen, Paulo Moura, Sabine Mayer, Ricardo Morales, Jorge Montilla, and the Clarinet Quartet from Caracas. Also, Luis Rossi, the Argentinian clarinetist and luthier who manufactures the instruments that have made me ever so happy since 1997.

Virgilio Vixama used to call the clarinet the "black stick," and he was serious, as if he spoke of something supernatural with mysterious reasons to be afraid of it.

"I am a *clarinetero*," he affirmed. "A clarinetist is something else."

He mentioned with almost religious respect the names of some good colleagues of Benny Goodman and Buddy DeFranco. The clarinet has a bad rap among the majority of saxophonists, because it's a much more delicate instrument and requires commitment to make it sound good. That is, it's very easy to make it sound horrible, even for great instrumentalists, even if only on a few occasions. If you play the clarinet, Yeyo, you must know what I'm talking about. You have to completely concentrate on it or it yells at you when you least expect it. It's like a jealous woman that demands absolute attention.

Phil Woods once told me, half joking and half serious, "My clarinet? It's been a lamp for a long time! That son of a bitch screams from inside the case."

Frank Wess insisted, "The clarinet was invented by five people who never met."

I think he was right.

Not that the saxophone is easy, it's not easy to play any instrument well, not even the kazoo. But at least that Belgian invention is much more reasonable and less demanding than the clarinet. That's why at the beginning of the 1960s, when saxophonists rediscovered the soprano sax, they were quickly convinced that by cultivating a nice tenor or alto sound, they could make the soprano sound like a Galician bagpipe or an Indian shehnai and that was "hip." The return of the soprano undoubtedly marked the end of the clarinet in jazz and popular music in general. Although, throughout the years, there have always been stubborn guys like Jimmy Giuffre, my dentists Phillip Terman and Ron Odrich, Kenny Davern, Don Byron, and a few more who keep imposing this black intruder on people.

Something has turned jazz clarinetists into a sort of impenetrable elite: they watch the "clarineteros" with terror and even with disdain. You can tell who they are, just by the way they take the instrument out of the case, by the way they put it together and put the reed in the mouthpiece. Believe me, when they blow (luckily it's never more than two or three notes), it sounds like the screaming of an owl or the badly greased brakes of a wagon axle.

"Where did you leave your alto?" is usually Jon Faddis's mandatory question, as soon as I get on the stage with him, and if I tell him that I left it at home, he looks at me as if he were constipated. I don't blame him, because I know the sound and potency of the saxophone go much better with bebop. We can't forget that in the 1940s, Buddy deFranco was the only clarinetist who struggled alone, in that magical world created by Dizzy, Monk, Bird, and Kenny Clarke. They could stand it because Buddy was the best, he was the one!

Without mentioning names or making enemies, there are saxophonists that made a career sounding horrible and way out of tune. The fans concentrate on any other virtue they can find: swing, creativity, ideas, you name it! And they turn them into musical geniuses.

I've spent my life trying to play this artifact in tune, and since I don't always do it, it torments me when I see colleagues who don't seem to be bothered by it or even try to go out of tune, thinking it has more swing. A radio presenter once told me that a certain saxophonist colleague didn't really play out of tune, but that he played sharp and flat at once. Since the program was recorded, I asked him to turn off the recorder and, looking at him straight in the eyes, I said slowly and clearly, "Listen to me, sir. Where I come from, playing sharp and flat at the same time is called playing out of tune, okay?"

New York, New York

If you can't find it in New York, then either it hasn't been invented or you don't need it.
—Maura Rivera, my mother

There are people whose names need not be mentioned for others to know who you are talking about. For example, when in the fabulous Cuban music scene of the 1940s and '50s they said, "The Maestro is conducting today!" everyone knew they were talking about Ernesto Lecuona. Or if they said, "The Only One," all the musicians would make the sign of the cross because they knew they had to accompany Rita Montaner. Rita had incredible graciousness and truly unique talents, but everyone who knew her says she wasn't a nice person.

It's the same in every culture: "The First Lady" (of jazz) is Ella Fitzgerald, "The Sound" is Stan Getz, and "The King" (of rock) was Elvis Presley.

For us "El Bárbaro" (of rhythm) is Benny Moré; "La Faraona," Lola Flores; "El Zorzal" (criollo), Gardel; "La Guarachera" (of Cuba), Celia Cruz; "The Deaf Man" (of Bonn), Beethoven; and "El Rey" (of timbales), Tito Puente. In Mexico everyone knows "La Doña" is María Félix and "El Flaco" is Agustín Lara.

Same thing happens with dictators. The Führer was "the Man of the Little Fly," and "Il Duce" was his Italian homologous (Benito Mussolini). What about Batista? "He's The Man," ass kissers and schmoozers of the shorthand-taking, sergeant-turned-president used to say.

You probably know this story, Yeyito. A man proclaimed throughout the streets of Havana, "That son of a bitch Fidel speaks today!"

Finally, a policeman grabs him by the arm, roughs him up, and spits on his face.

"You are under arrest for defamation of the Commander in Chief."

"But, compañero officer, there are many people called Fidel," replies the detainee.

And so the agent responds, "True, but there's only one who is a son of a bitch!"

See that? It's the best example of the man, given by his own people.

Talking geography, Puerto Rico is "The Island of Charm," and Cuba is "The Pearl of the Antilles." They say "from Madrid to heaven," Paris is "The City of Lights," and Vienna, "the City of Waltzes." Although, "I left my heart in San Francisco" (as Tony Bennett sings), Cienfuegos is the city that I like the best (as Benny Moré sang).

However, above all those mentioned above, although it's well known as "The Big Apple," "The Big One," or the "Asphalt Jungle," all you have to say is "The City." The mind instantly conjures thousands of people of all races, tall skyscrapers, a parade of fast-driving yellow taxis, the smell of foods from every corner of the world, and the accelerated rhythm and swagger of New York City. As Sinatra said, "It's such a tremendous city, you have to say its name twice!"

You don't have to be born in New York to be a New Yorker! Duke Ellington and Leonard Bernstein, two of the most representative composers of the city, were born in other states, just like a great number of its inhabitants. To be a New Yorker is more like a mental state—one of many ways to act, an attitude towards life and the rest of the world. Many people say the planet is divided in two: New York and the rest of the world.

The first time I heard about New York it was from my father. It was the day he brought home a record that changed my life forever. A Silverstone portable record player in a case, which he had bought at Sears in Marianao, replaced the phonograph that my old man Tito (who wasn't old then) played 78-RPM Ellington, Al Gallodoro, Marcel Moise, Artie Shaw, Mario Lanza, and Lester Young records. That afternoon, he brought a plaque on a multicolor jacket with six pictures of a clarinetist with the heading "The Great Benny Goodman." The names of Harry James, Gene Krupa, Teddy Wilson, Lionel Hampton, and many other great jazz artists were highlighted in red, black, and blue letters. Tito placed the LP over the revolving dish of the machine that still smelled like new and put the needle almost on the edge, over the striped surface of the vinyl record. The soft murmur produced for a few seconds by the friction of the minute metallic point on the virgin plastic accented my curiosity of the unknown even more. Every time a new record made it to our home I would prepare for a totally different adventure. Right away this time we heard the notes of "Let's Dance," Benny Goodman's orchestra's musical theme. The solid rhythmic section seemed to be like the root and the trunk of a strong, healthy tree. On it, the tight saxophone section bloomed exuberantly, like springtime. The trumpets splashed the melody like fresh dew and suddenly stopped to let Benny's crystal-clear, playful sound step right in. Like a bird of light, his song ascended, stroking the sparkling stars. My God! That band moved as smoothly as a dinghy down the Hudson.

Many years later, producer John Avakian, who wrote the notes of the superb recording that didn't come out until 1956, told me that the theme was arranged by mastermind Fletcher Henderson, who had written it for the popular radio show "Let's Dance." The theme was based on the celebrated "Invitation to Waltz" by Karl María von Weber.

Extremely impressed by what I heard, when the first side of the record was over I asked my dad, "What was that?"

He answered with a mischievous smile: "Swing! The Benny Goodman Orchestra at Carnegie Hall."

The sound of Carnegie Hall was almost like "carne y frijol." Surprised by the relationship my mother's cooking could have with such inspired music, I asked, "Did you say 'meat and beans'?"

My old man cracked up laughing but finally calmed down and described Benny, swing, Carnegie Hall, and the amazing city where its red brick columns were erected. He spoke about Jascha Heifetz, Rubinstein, Rachmaninoff, Caruso, and all the great artists that had performed there since the end of the nineteenth century. He later spoke of the Broadway theaters,

Harlem, the Apollo Theater, and the Savoy, where the memorable big band battles took place. He told me about the time Goodman and Chick Webb's bands played together. He also mentioned Mario Bauzá, who in 1928, at age seventeen, dove into the New York adventure and in a few years joined them and was even musical director of Noble Sissle, Chick Webb, and Cab Calloway's orchestras until he founded Machito & his Afro-Cubans. I could tell in my dad's voice how deep his admiration was for Mario. He showed me a catalogue from Martin Instruments, where there was a photograph of Mario Bauzá with his trumpet, along with other pictures of Buck Clayton, Bobby Hackett, Ziggy Elman, and other famous musicians.

My dad declared, "Mario had a vision, a dream, my little son; he went where he had to go to find it, and so he did! That's how it's done."

There are those who assure that the first piece of the genre we know today as Latin jazz was "Tanga," written by Mario.

Since that time, New York became an obsession for me. From that very day, as my dad enhanced his record collection, he also enriched my young mind with music by Benny Goodman, Dizzy Gillespie, Paul Desmond, Bernstein, Charlie Parker, Gershwin, Nat King Cole, Count Basie, and many other American musicians. Since then, I dreamed of developing my career in the same town that opened its generous concrete and steel heart to so many artists from all over the world. Years later, after traveling the globe, I would conclude there isn't another city like this one, not even in the United States.

I remember once I got on the legendary A train to Harlem, the famous subway immortalized by Billy Strayhorn in his "Take the A Train" recording with Duke Ellington's band. At one of the stops, a guy came in holding a tenor saxophone. He was short, with indigenous features and was wearing a cap with the colors and star of the Puerto Rican flag. Raising his voice and lifting the instrument, he said, "Ladies and gentlemen, please pay attention. I have something to communicate to you. I play this artifact, terribly bad, but I have a critical financial situation and a family to support." The passengers on the train looked at each other without ever imagining where he was going with this, while the man continued. "What I want to say is, I recommend you contribute generously to alleviate my unstable situation with any amount you might be able to. That way, it will not be necessary for me to blow on this thing, because, I repeat, I make it sound horrible!"

The man concluded, and we all laughed out loud. Our unanimous laughter echoed all over. At the end we all dug into our pockets and contributed so this man, who was supposedly as bad a musician as he was a loquacious and humorous street comedian, could put a hot meal on his family's table.

As I stepped down from the subway on One Hundred-and-something Street, I saw a young skinny black man, smiling mischievously, sitting on a wooden bench, and smoking a cigarette that looked way too skinny to be made out of tobacco. He wore a colorful knit hat like Bob Marley would have worn and sandals that he seemed to have walked in from Kingston. Across from him, on the sidewalk, he had on a wooden easel a cardboard sign that read in black ink, "I NEED AN URGENT PENIS REDUCTION. THANK YOU." At the bottom of the easel, there was a can with a few dollars and coins that he himself had probably put in as a hook.

A beautiful mixed-race girl walked by the corner. She had a bigger afro than Angela Davis's and tons of charm overflowing from her pores. She was wearing very high, red stilettos, very tight jeans, and a transparent Indian blouse that revealed small, powerful breasts.

"Hi, Fikisha!" said the young man, greeting the café-au-lait beauty with a hint of complicity or irony in his baritone voice. The girl stopped and looked him over with her caramel eyes. Ignoring his greeting, she glanced at the sign and read it slowly out loud in a medium voice, word by word.

"'I need money for an urgent penis reduction,'" she read, strongly emphasizing in the word "reduction," where she paused. Then she squinted, made an unmistakable gesture of skepticism, and, addressing the unusual beggar, she said, repulsively, "You liar!" Then with her African princess walk, she turned around and continued strolling down the street as if all of Harlem belonged to her. The guy hid behind the colorful hat, and I thought, "Shit! Things like this only happen in New York! Isn't that so?"

For those of you who haven't yet read *My Sax Life*, the first time I came to New York was in April 1960, to perform in the Teatro Puerto Rico with Rolando Laserie, Celia Cruz, Lola Beltrán, and a magnificent orchestra conducted by Puerto Rican trumpet player César Concepción. I was twelve. From the time I stepped off the plane and saw a black man driving a Cadillac I thought, "Hmmm, this is where I want to live!"

During that time, a friend of my old man that I admired not only as a musician but also because of his special qualities and sharp way of dressing was already living in New York. Among the many other great things I inherited from my dad was the great friendship of Alfredo "Chocolate" Armenteros, a true symbol of Cuban music among Cuban musicians.

Chocolate was with us almost the whole time we stayed in the city of skyscrapers. He took us around the marvelous jungle that had been my childhood dream since the afternoon Tito brought home the Benny Goodman album. Now I could better understand those solos by Krupa, Hampton, and Teddy Wilson, blending with the sounds of that gigantic and passionate town where Benny's clarinet sounded so alive. I was at a point where I didn't know if it was all true or part of my obsessive dream. Or is it perhaps that New York itself is an obsessive dream?

Chocolate must have caught on to how impressed I was and pulled me out of my trance by asking me with his typical charm, "Well, partner, tell me what you think of 'The Big One,' won't you?"

I was frankly in such a shock that I shrugged, not knowing what to say. Even today, after so many years living here, I sometimes think it's all a dream, since only in dreams do you see things that happen here on a daily basis. It's true that in this city reality exceeds the most fantastic fiction.

My mother, a staunch New Yorker, says that whatever you don't find in New York has not yet been invented or you just don't need it. Once, my good friend, Finnish pianist and conductor Esko Linnavalli, said while he checked out *The Village Voice*, "Whatever happens in this town (culturally) in one day, happens in any other world capital in a whole year."

In New York you can have the best Japanese lunch in any of the many sushi bars in town then sip a great espresso in Starbucks on your way to the Museum of Modern Art, where you'll enjoy an exhibition of contemporary Mongolian paintings, then stop at a matinee of the American Ballet company, where they might have Alicia Alonso or Fernando Bujones as special guest. (Or both. You never know, pal, this is New York.)

As you come out of the ballet, you have enough time to decide between Pavarotti and Plácido Domingo (singing or conducting the orchestra) at the Metropolitan Opera House, or perhaps a zarzuela at the Repertorio Español. Maybe you prefer the New York Philharmonic under Lorin Mazel, or the Mostly Mozart Festival (once a year at Lincoln Center). Later on, a tasteful Brazilian dinner at Via Brasil and then to the Village to listen to great jazz at any of the many clubs in the bohemian neighborhood, where the same night you can pick between Herbie Hancock and Joe Lovano, passing through Kenny Barron, Pat Metheny, Danilo Pérez, Jon Faddis, or the Count Basie or Chick Corea orchestras.

A night of good music is not complete unless you dance a little salsa, let's say at the Copacabana salsa club, where it is very possible you'll find Eddie Palmieri or El Gran Combo de Puerto Rico, or both. (You never know, pal, *this* is New York!)

After that visit in 1960, it would be eighteen years before I returned to the Big Apple—first to record an album with Irakere and then as a curtain act for Stephen Stills. That tour around many cities and towns of the east and a Grammy Awards presentation in Los Angeles (considered by some a plastic, artificial city) helped convince me of two fundamental things: that New York is much more than the United States, and that there was a place there for me.

We came back the next year, and, as they say, the third time is the charm. On October 23, 1980, after staying a little more than five months in charming Madrid, I finally achieved my childhood goal and established myself in the Asphalt Jungle. There was truly a place for me here, as there is for anyone with the essential determination and adaptability to build a life in this jungle of opportunities, difficulties, caresses, and scratches.

I can't get out of my mind, the time upon my arrival here, strolling through the heart of "La City," when I heard from far away a jazz group playing with such energy, precision, and creativity that it sounded like the recording of a famous group. Still, I couldn't recognize the saxophonist's style. This was happening on the sidewalk of what was Virgin Records in Times Square.

A large group of people gathered around what turned out to be a street combo, a trio of bass, drums, and a young extraordinary alto saxophonist that got sparks out of the instrument. Confused by the quality of the street musicians, I continued my leisurely walk in the New York spring around Times Square. A few blocks down they had an international food fair all through Ninth Avenue. On the corner, by an Arab falafel stand, I found another trio, as interesting as the first one, more because of its original format: bass, drums, and a bassoonist that had his instrument connected to a small amplifier. It was the first time I ever heard anyone play bebop phrases on an instrument like the bassoon, which up until that day was the antithesis of "swing."

I continued making my way through the area known as Hell's Kitchen with crowds of people. Although I am not quite a puritan, I was shocked going up Forty-Second Street by the filth, the sordid porno joints, and drug vendors in an area where, during my visit in 1960, there were only lights, healthy tourism, movies, and theaters on both sides of the street. I walked by the massive green building that houses the bus terminal and crossed Eighth Avenue. At the entrance of the same theater where years before there was a clown selling sugar candy, there was a dark bearded man in a floor-length white tunic by a table of incense sticks and oriental fragrances. I saw a thin, clumsy, dirty, colorless guy with long hair and an absent look in his eyes, Walking fast and nervously, up and down the street, mumbling "smoke, smoke!" I later found out he was selling dope.

Moved by curiosity, I entered one of those small stores with windows lit by neon lights and tiny round mirrors, displaying water pipes and all sorts of paraphernalia to smoke marijuana, crack, and anything else smoke-able. They also sold thin silver tubes to inhale cocaine and minute amber-colored bottles with teeny spoons on top to carry the Andean Snow. They had accessories for any existing drug and also for those not yet invented. They had everything but hypodermic needles, which were totally forbidden by law before the AIDS crisis.

"Excuse me, sir. What is this for?" I asked a very short man, almost a midget, with tattoos all over his body. He looked like a Caribbean Indian and seemed to either work there or own the store. The man was wearing bright red high heel boots and old worn out jeans so full of holes he looked like a veteran of a John Wayne movie. He also wore a muscle shirt with Mao Tse Tung's face with huge ears that read "Mickey-Mao." His head was as long as a football, and his shiny, black hair was combed into a ponytail and held by a fluorescent elastic band.

Adhered to the elastic band he had a long feather, seemingly from a huge bird. "Shit! This midget must be the punk grandson of Hatuey!" I thought, smiling to myself.

The guy must have read my mind, because he approached me in a grave, deep voice that contrasted with his minimal size and, I suppose in response to my beans-and-rice accent, said in perfect Spanish, "The one with the strainer in the metallic color is to smoke grass, or even better to smoke hashish. And this large crystal one is a water pipe, great for crack. Which one would you like, brother?"

"None, thanks," I replied. "I just thought that all these were illegal."

He looked me in the eye. Maybe he thought I was an undercover cop or something. Then he laughed out loud, revealing his shining gold teeth. Still laughing, he said, "Illeeeegal! No brother! There is nothing illegal here! Drugs are illegal, not these little accouterments to use them." He looked around and lowered his heavy voice. Standing in his toes to reach my ear, he mumbled, "But if you want, you can get anything here, my brother. Okay? Just ask for whatever you need, and I am the one and only Aladdin."

"No, thank you, brother. Goodbye," I said and rushed up the street, mixing with the crowd.

"Smoke, smoke, got dat weed," continued the untidy, skinny guy, monotonously. I still had playing in my head the young saxophonist's improvisations and the bassoonist that played beautifully. When I got to the island formed by Broadway and Seventh Avenue between Forty-Second and Forty-Third streets, I stopped to admire the impressive group of buildings in Times Square from that angle. The lid of the gigantic Coca Cola bottle that was on top of the Forty-Eighth Street building (where they used to sell musical instruments and accessories) still lifted itself automatically in those days. Under the ad of the most popular drink in the world, the Castro Convertibles sign brought me bad memories.

"Nah! Cuban exile traumas," I thought, laughing at my own paranoia.

A couple of buses went by, the red kind with two stories, like the ones that carry tourists all over London. Over there they go to Piccadilly Circus and Buckingham Palace, in Paris to the Eiffel Tower, and here to the Empire State Building and the Statue of Liberty. Tourists do pretty much the same thing everywhere.

On the opposite side of the street, I saw a man dressed in an Andean outfit with high wool socks, a poncho, and a hat with earmuffs. He was talking to a mounted policeman. The man had something that looked like a *charango* in his hand. A charango is an Andean musical instrument with five double strings, generally made from an armadillo's shell. Next to the native guy, his lama ate and drank from a couple of plastic pails on the sidewalk.

Possibly prompted by the curious policeman, the man pulled out his instrument and filled the New York afternoon with the nostalgic and distant sounds of the Andean high plateau. A few minutes later, a Japanese tourist with his camera hanging from his neck stopped. He pulled a bamboo flute from his pocket and joined his oriental melody to the charango player's strumming.

I got closer to the crowd that swiftly gathered around them to listen to the inspired sounds improvised by those two beings from opposite extremes of the world who had never before seen each other. They played for a long time, and when they finished, the crowd applauded frantically. The musicians were jumping with joy. They hugged each other euphorically, something as out of character for Asians as for those who come from the Andean mountains. It was the magic power of music, the true universal language.

"Me, Take Yamamoto, Japan, *domo arigato*," said the tourist, speaking like a Japanese Tarzan, bowing in reverence, and trying to exchange words that none of them understood. But who cared? The music had said it all. The huge brown horse let out a neigh, and the group scattered.

"*Sayonara*," said the street musician trying to say goodbye to the tourist. He took a picture of the policeman on horseback with the Andean friend and his exotic animal. Then, he continued his blissful stroll towards Forty-Second Street and Fifth Avenue. The mounted policeman continued patrolling the streets. The lama finished eating and wandered down Broadway with the smiling mountain man. Both seemed to be swathed in a peaceful cloud.

"Jesus is coming, Jesus is coming! Repent now for all your sins!" shouted a preacher wearing a suit and tie. More than a message of hope it sounded like a threat. "Repent sinner! Our Lord is coming soon!" Next to him a silent sad woman held a Bible high, while with the other hand she dragged a little boy by his wrist. The boy, in a man's costume, looked like a ventriloquist's dummy. Not far from them a filthy looking hippy couple that seemed frozen in the '60s joined passionately in an unending kiss. By their feet a little poodle of indefinite color scratched furiously all over. As the couple passed by, a sour, dated stench could be smelled. But it was impossible to determine if the smell came from the couple, the dog, or the supermarket cart loaded with the diverse junk they hauled.

I continued on Sixth and crossed the avenue. I went to the park behind the public library with the huge lions on the steps. There, I bumped into a guy that played two alto saxophones at the same time. They were united in the lower extreme by a common bell. The musician had obviously invented the artifact. He reminded me of Rahsaan Roland Kirk. He was accompanied by a bassist I don't quite remember and a very young *jabaíta* with yellowish braids that played phenomenally well in a style that took me back to Tony Williams.

"Go, Irakere!" said a voice behind me. I felt a soft pat on my back, turned around, and bumped into a young mullato I didn't know but whose accent was very familiar. He had stepped down from his bike taking off his helmet. He wore a tight blue and yellow sport cyclist suit and from his right shoulder hung a plastic messenger's bag. He said he was a Marielito, a Cuban that made it to the Florida coasts in mid-1980. He probably came in a one of the vessels that left the port of Mariel, a few kilometers from Havana, authorized by Fidel Castro. During the Marielazo more than 125,000 compatriots left Cuba in three months. That number doesn't account for those who died in the ocean, due to vessels that were dangerously overloaded.

"You don't know me. But I never missed any of those Monday jams at Johnny's Dream with Emiliano Salvador, Negro Nicolás, Carlitos Puerto, and Enrique Plá. I'm not a musician, but you guys taught me the fascinating world of improvisation. I think that's why when Mariel happened, I decided to come up here and establish myself in New York, where jazz walks the streets and you can breathe it in the air."

The man had followed me from the days of the Cuban Modern Music Orchestra and the Irakere Group, until my first presentations in the Big Apple at Verna Gillis's Soundscape. On that fifth floor of Fifty-Second and Tenth Avenue with Jorge Dalto, Daniel Ponce, Cláudio Roditi, the brothers Jerry and Andy González, Mario Rivera, and Hilton Ruiz.

"Who's the guy with the weird instrument and the dynamic jabaíta that plays like Tony Williams?" I asked the Cuban in love with jazz and New York.

"Ooooohhhh! That's George Braithwaite, a typical New York musician who recorded several albums for Blue Note and Prestige in the sixties. He even founded a jazz club called Musart. Then he went to Europe for a while. Now he plays in the streets, because they say he got fed up with dealing with that fucked-up music business. It happened to many musicians before, like Artie Shaw during the fifties, for example, at the height of his career."

With just a few words, the cubiche displayed his impressive historical knowledge of music.

"And what about the weird machine?" I wanted to know.

"The thing is that Braith (he's shortened his name) was influenced by Roland Kirk and used to blow a soprano with a Strich, which as you know, is a straight alto. So, he later invented the machine he calls Braithophone and unites two sopranos to a common bell. It's interesting…right? And the jabaíta you like is Cindy Blackman, I think. I tell you again, man, I'm not a musician, but I'm sure that she'll be the talk of the town someday. I'll see you later, Irakere. My lunch hour is over, and I have to go back to work."

And with that, my fellow Cuban put on his helmet shaped like a mamey, got on his bike, and disappeared into Forty-Second's convoluted traffic without even giving me time to ask his name.

While I listened to the intrinsic musical maze Braith's musicians escaped to, I got a little worried. I thought, "Hell, if these are the prodigies that play in the street, I don't even want to know what the ones in the musicians' union sound like."

How could I have imagined then that the saxophonist and the bassoonist who so impressed me that afternoon in mid-1981 were none other than Vincent Herring and Michael Rabinowitz, who would go on to have brilliant careers in the world of jazz a while later.

Then I learned that many young artists practiced in the streets of New York. People contribute by placing coins and dollars in the open instrument case, and that's how they pay their rent and for private or conservatory lessons.

Many of these walking talents even have licenses, and if they're good, they make a lot of money trying to penetrate the competitive American professional scene. In the '90s I met a Peruvian flutist they call "El Vate" for his ability to write poems. This peculiar character plays *quenas, zampoñas,* and all other original flutes from the Andes Mountains, and he produces his own records. He hires famous musicians and pays them well for their work. He tours American cities, playing the streets and selling his records, earning a real fortune with his work. Once, when I hadn't seen him for a long time, I bumped into him in Times Square. He had been to the Olympics in Atlanta, where he stayed at a five-star hotel, went to many sports events, played near the stadium, and sold all the records he took with him. I was the guest artist on one of them.

When people live in the streets of New York, their lives are enriched with invaluable experiences, memories, and anecdotes. Like this delicious story my friend El Vate tells here in his own words:

When Indian Yovanny and I arrived in downtown Manhattan that afternoon, it was the spring of 1988. We were in the Astor Place area, where we had an Argentine friend in a Broadway beauty salon. He always asked us to play near his business, and upon his repeated insistence we decided to do a small presentation with Yovanny on guitar and me playing the flutes. We began to play in the subtlest and most relaxing way possible, and immediately an audience gathered around us and started buying our cassettes.

We kept playing very softly, when all of a sudden, a noisy window opens up and a fat, old woman starts screaming, "Damned unfortunate Indians, stop playing your damn music and beat it! I hate you! Shut up already!"

When we saw such offensive action towards us, we decided to connect the amplifiers and started playing really loud, almost unbearably.

The woman showed her head out the window again and said, "Damn Indians! So you want to kill me. Now you will see!" and she disappeared.

She didn't come back out, so we continued with the music. Around fifteen minutes later, when we had the most people gathered around us, two police patrol cars on the wrong side of the street and a van with four policemen on the other side came down Broadway and parked next to us. The policemen stepped out of the cars, guns in hand. The audience spread out immediately. I started to put away my instruments and the amplifier in my small handcart. Since I didn't speak good English back then, I let Yovanny, who is an Ecuadorian, raised by Native Americans in New York City, handle the mess. He really knew how to deal with the police. He starts arguing that we were Native Americans and it wasn't fair, after taking our land away, that they now wanted to take our art too. When he said that, all the policemen's jaws dropped; they were not only surprised but also hypnotized by the character speaking.

I already had my things packed and ready to go and started leaving right in front of them, as any other pedestrian would. The police kept listening to everything Yovanny said.

When I got to the barber shop the Argentine said, "Have a seat and I will cut your hair."

I sat down still scared. The barber put my things in a small room and after a few seconds the police realized I was gone. They arrest Yovanny and start a huge police operation to find me. A few minutes later, one of them comes in asking the hairdresser if anyone had come in with a suitcase full of musical instruments and an amplifier. The Argentine says absolutely not, as he was cutting my hair. Around twenty minutes later I went home.

Moral of the story: A free Indian is better than two in custody.

Since I heard this story, I have felt respect and empathy for those street musicians that bring art and happiness to the Asphalt Jungle that is New York City. And even if I don't like what they're playing, I go deep into my pockets and leave them a good tip, especially after what I went through in Miami one night in the early '80s.

The Take Five Lounge of Miami's Airport Inn was one of the few jazz places in Miami those days. They had a very good local band directed by pianist Billy Marcus. Every night drummer Gary Duchaine, saxophonist Eric Allison, bassist Steve (El Pelúo) Bailey, and singer Sandy Patton played with him. Sandy, who was for years with Lionel Hampton, later became the professor of jazz voice at a prestigious conservatory in Bern, Switzerland.

Steve Bailey, who worked and recorded with me and later on with Dizzy Gillespie, became "El Pelúo" because of the blonde, untidy hair that made him resemble a caveman. With that excellent group, they accompanied soloists brought in every week from all over the US. They invited me back several times. One time was when they gave me the key to the city, during carnival time. Since then, they have continued to celebrate *"carnavales"* every year, all along popular Calle Ocho, in the heart of southwest Miami, better known as "La Saguesera." I was invited another time, either 1983 or 1984.

The club was full to capacity, and, as is customary, most of us men were wearing tuxedos. My instruments were on top of two sax stands on stage where Marcus's quintet had played several tunes to warm up the house. I remember that Sandy and Eric (who also sang with great swing) had just finished singing a duet of "Don't Get Around Much Any More," a song I love, from Helen Humes's repertory. In the meantime, I waited for my turn to play behind the dark door at the right end of the establishment.

While the rhythm section played the intro vamp to Adolfo Guzmán's "Al Fin Amor," which was my opening theme then, Eric Allison said from stage, "Ladies and gentlemen, the Take Five Lounge is proud to present Paquito D'Rivera."

The audience started to applaud, and I walked towards the stage, blending with the waiters who like me, were wearing tuxedos. As I walked by the bar to the side of the nightclub, a strong, deafening, sharp whistle was heard way above the orchestra and the audience's applause. It came from a table close by.

When I looked that way I saw a big guy, wearing a bunch of gold chains hanging over his hairy chest. With the low temperature they always kept in the room, he gave me the impression of a polar bear dipped in a pool of Clairol hair dye. He had no room for any more gold or precious stone rings on his fat hairy hands. His sunglasses in the club's dimness were a surrealist anachronism. He was wearing cowboy boots, gleaming spurs and all. They actually shined under the table. Brown leather pants (probably boiling his balls) in the Miami heat completed the troglodyte's outfit.

"Hey you!" he called. "Yes, you," the loud *cubanazo* yelled at me, gesticulating boldly next to his exuberant brunette date. Under his black bushy moustache he held a huge cigar that resembled the Olympic torch. In those days it was still legal to suffocate your fellow men with nicotine. The subject in question was wearing a colorful, half-opened Hawaiian shirt that revealed his gorilla chest above his leather pants.

His chest was like a sea of black curls, where the gold vessel of "the three Juanes" floated, embellished by emeralds under the guarding image of La Virgen de la Caridad. His date wore a silver miniskirt exposing a set of golden thighs that would turn Jennifer López green with envy. Her cleavage went down to her belly button and her eyelashes aired out my face as a gazelle in the woods would. She had an evening purse resting on her lap with the words "I LOVE NEW YORK" embroidered in colorful rhinestones.

I hesitated for a minute before I got close to the beauty and the beast. "Can I help you, sir?" I asked in my best English. He answered as if he was sitting at the Rumba Palace Nightclub in a lowdown row of Havana clubs.

"Look, bro, throw a couple of very cold Heinekens this way," he said with the smoking torch between his lips.

"Of course, sir," I said, bowing and heading towards the corner of the bar where waiters got their drinks. I ordered and paid for the beers on behalf of the Cuba-non-sapiens. I then delivered them.

The group kept playing. People had stopped applauding and were now immersed in Billy Marcus's four-hundred-pound jam over his frantic piano solo.

"Don't we even get glasses here, partner?" protested the guy, upset and impatient.

"Oh excuse me, sir, I'm not accustomed to, that" I said, and brought two frozen mugs from the bar, along with paper napkins. I served the foaming yellow liquid smoothly in the lady's glass, while I underhandedly took a glance at her nerve-racking thighs from sideways and stoically put up with the nauseating polluted smoke from the Cro-Magnon man's cigar.

"Tell me how much I owe you, big man," said the voice, shaking me out from my dream.

"Nothing, sir, nothing. It's on the house. Happy new year," I said affectionately. As I continued my way to stage, just a bit disconcerted, I could feel his puzzled look for not understanding my courtesy.

I finally got to the proscenium, stepped on the multicolor light, lifted my saxophone from its stand, and hung it from my neck. The audience applauded with enthusiasm. I glanced at the panoramic view of the place, recognizing familiar faces, among them comedian Guillermo Álvarez Guedes, the multi-instrumentalist Ira Sullivan, and journalist Norma Niurka. When I looked at the table where I had served the beers I saw a cloud of smoke and soaring sparks.

The Cro-Magnon man was standing on his feet, his eyes wide open looking straight at me. The cigar had fallen to the floor and his jaw had dropped to his chest, while the brunette with the golden thighs and long eyelashes was cracking up on the chair holding her I Love NY purse. I saw her get up afterwards and gesticulate as if reprimanding her date. Then she disappeared between smoke and shadows.

That image has stayed in my mind for a long time, and I always tell the story of the cubanazo who ordered the two Heineken beers minutes before my performance in a Miami club.

Back to the Asphalt Jungle, on West Forty-First Street by the Manhattan bus station, there was a famous rehearsal studio called Carroll Music. Just next to it was the Savoy Bar, where musicians used to freshen up during intermission. It was the 1983 summer concert season of the Brooklyn

Philharmonic in Prospect Park. So while David Amram re-hearsed a Mozart symphony and I waited my turn, I went to the Savoy to have a very cold Beck's beer.

I was surprised to see that the bar was almost deserted. Just a couple of clients talked in a very low tone at the other extreme of the long wooden counter. Another two clients played a game of pool under the discreet light on the other end. Instead of the usual Italian bartender, there was a very tall, corpulent woman with a leather belt over her white silk shirt with huge black spots. Under it, you could discern the gigantic tits of a Dutch cow. Little golden chains hung from the vest, and on the other side she had a golden police badge. She was wearing leather pants that matched the vest and cowboy boots with silver spurs. The small diamond on her ear shined in the shadows. She had a red scarf knotted on her head, hiding part of a very black and abundant head of hair. Another red scarf hung from the back pocket of her leather pants, completed the gay outfit. Or at least that's what it seemed to me.

I remember the song "Patricia" by the King of Mambo, Dámaso Pérez Prado's Mexican Orchestra, was playing. The woman kept getting closer slowly, looking insistently at me, a bit puzzled. The spurs of her boots added a sound effect when the mysterious being walked from side to side. So, when she finally got to me, she redirected her eyes a bit, and before she could ask what I wanted, I asked for a beer. She served it without mentioning a word, and I noticed something familiar in this person's look. She reminded me of someone or something, which made me for some reason a little nervous. I drank the beer up and asked for my bill.

"Don't worry, this time it's on me," the grave but feminine voice said in perfect Spanish. She was smiling insistently with her piercing eyes on me. I neither understood a thing nor tried to. I left a dollar on top of the bar and rushed out the closest door. I walked swiftly towards Carroll's. Almost reaching the studio, I turned around and glanced at the bar where I had been a few minutes before. I noticed they had changed the sign outside. It was now called "HOMBRE," just like that and in Spanish. They had turned it into a gay bar!

Right at that moment the Tit-o-sarous with the spurs and leather suit was calling me from the door, waving the cover of an LP pretty high. I had no other choice than to return and sign the cover of my album *Mariel*, my third recording for CBS.

"I am a Marielito also, you know? And I'm very happy about your successes," he said affectionately when I returned the autographed album cover. Then he told me he had finally released the woman kept prisoner in his man's body practically all his life and had moved to New York where he had the complicated sex change surgery. She missed Cuba a lot, but she was happy with her new identity. I kind of saw a black cloud darken her face when she said this, so I told her I would also like to change my sex.

"Oh! Are you a homosexual too?" she asked, quite horrified.

"No," I answered. "But I would like to change mine for a bigger one." It made her laugh a lot!

She ended up saying that she was now Maria, but before she had been Mario, the cubanazo who had ordered the beers at Miami's Take Five. She was now returning the courtesy I had shown. What an incredible story! When I said goodbye to Maria, I thought, "Damn! Only in New York! Isn't that right?"

$$$

It was when I arrived in New York, back in 1980, that my Cuban-American girlfriend, Carmenchú Santana Vega, who was raised in the US, suddenly said to me one evening, as we were stepping out of a Manhattan restaurant, "McFlaco, you always have to find the economic equivalent of your work. That's how it is here."

And Carmenchú was right, also keeping in mind that in our profession, as in life, there are things that all the money in the world can't buy.

Like the time when a guy stopped me on Union City's Bergenline Street, where many Cubans used to live a while back.

"Listen, musician," he said. "There's a patriotic act this weekend, and the Cubans want you to play a little. We don't have a lot of money, a hundred dollars more or less. But the good part is, you only have to play about eight-to-ten minutes."

It made me laugh, and the only thing I could think to ask him was, "On top of not paying me, are you thinking of not letting me play either?"

But the guy didn't understand. It's not his world, and he doesn't have to understand that for us, the nightmare ends when the music starts.

My old Guantanamero friend Pucho Escalante, trombonist and protagonist of my novel *Oh, La Habana!*, always tells me that in the 1940s and '50s Cuban musicians had great admiration for Gilberto Valdés, the genius who wrote "Og-guere," "Baró," and "El botellero." With the enthusiasm of fifty years back still in his eyes, blue as the sky, he said to me, "Paquito, Gilberto was unique! His music seemed to have just arrived in Havana on a boat from Africa. And he expressed it in a *charanga* as well as the Philharmonic!"

That sort of thing was more common among *rumberos*, the ones who played with "feeling," or people of the night in general. This happened much more so with jazz people during the famous jam sessions, when, after finishing their theater or concert gigs, musicians went to any club where there was a piano and a set of drums and jammed until daybreak. In 1967, for example, was the first Cuban Popular Song Festival in Varadero, which took place right on the shore of that beautiful beach.

When Georgia was part of the USSR, the great Georgian singer Giuli Chokheli came to the festival. She was an enchanting enigmatic beauty who came with her husband, the extraordinary Russian pianist Boris Richkov, the writer of all her arrangements for the festival's orchestra. Every night at the end of the concerts, everyone went to hang out at the ample bar of the International Hotel. There was an upright piano and a drum set Enrique Plá had put in there for the jam sessions. To make a long story short, after everyone was tired of playing, Russian Boris, who played in style similar to Oscar Peterson, would sit at the piano, a glass of vodka filled to the top, with Cachaíto on the contrabass (no amplifier) and Enrique glued to his brushes, and they didn't move from there until daybreak. And it went on for the whole week of the event.

But it doesn't only happen with jazz musicians. I remember during the beautiful tour celebrating *Obrigado Brazil* with Yo-Yo Ma, someone got us the parts of Johannes Brahms's trio for clarinet, cello, and piano so that we could have fun playing something other than what we played every evening.

And it's true, the rent and the bills have to be paid, and jam sessions don't solve that, nor do chamber music reunions at friends' homes or hotel rooms or dressing rooms. It is true that music is an art, but in our case it's a profession first, a service we have to put a price on, or we starve! Besides, music tastes best when it comes with a nice check (and better yet if it's cash) so that we can invite our wives and friends to have a whiskey or a decent meal at Manhattan's Victor's Café on Fifty-Second and Broadway.

Usually there's a little bargaining from the promoter's side, and generally there's a margin to negotiate a fair pay according to our merits and power of attracting people to hear our abilities or according to the quality and demand for our service, in the case that we accompany a main soloist. We must learn, Yeyito, fair remuneration on both sides, and no one better than ourselves should know the fair price of each occasion. It changes from one place to the other, keeping in mind the size of the venue, the price of tickets, even distance and rest time. This is not an easy business, but no business is really easy, and since we do this, we have to learn as much as we can about the business.

We don't need to exaggerate or put the promoter or the bandleader in an unbearable situation. Something very funny happened with Cachao and Charlie Fishman, whom we affectionately call "El Pescao" (The Fish). Bebo Valdés told me the story, and the thing is, he said Cachao liked dollars very much (who doesn't?) and would sometimes get greedy. As Bebo explained, El Pescao had gotten a considerable fee for the orchestra in a New York club, and when Cachao heard the figure, he widened his eyes like an owl.

"Good, that's for me," he said to Charlie. "Now what are you going to pay the musicians?"

Another useful detail is the nationality, like for example, Brazilians, whom, as we said before, have millions of followers of their marvelous culture around the world. And in our case, Yeyo, being Cuban can be an attractive factor for some. From the middle of the nineteenth century on, Cuban music and musicians enjoyed great prestige in diverse fields of the music industry. Cuban music professionals have singled themselves out inside the trade, like José White, Claudio Brindis de Salas, Ignacio Cervantes, Ernesto Lecuona, Alberto Socarrás, Olga Guillot, Mario Bauzá, Alberto Bolet, Leo Brouwer, Chico O'Farrill, and Jorge Luis Prats, to mention just a few.

They give Cuban musicians diverse genres and musical styles not common in other nationalities, which tend to apply themselves to just one activity. No other nation has been as musically influential as Cuba has been. That may sound a bit arrogant, but to Caesar what is rightfully his.

In New York, there are several American musicians who are loyal cultivators of Cuban and Latin music in general. Shortly after I established myself in New York, I got a call from saxophonist Mitch Forman. Mitch always had a lot to do with Latino musicians in New York and worked for years with Tito Puente. He sometimes organized a sort of small big band with two trumpets, a trombone, three saxophones, and a powerful Latin jazz rhythmic section.

Even if the pay was disastrous, the arrangements were high quality and we had a lot of fun playing. For that reason, the small band sometimes gathered brilliant musicians attracted by the Jewish saxophonist's orchestrations, like Cláudio Roditi, Andy and Jerry González, Jon Faddis, Conrad Herwig, and Bobby Porcelli. The first time Mitch called me, we hadn't met personally, but my Dominican friend, saxophonist Mario Rivera, told him about me and we agreed to meet at the Home Restaurant, a very small place on Manhattan's First Avenue, where miraculously, there was enough space for customers, waiters, and Mitch's orchestra. The agreed-upon pay was five dollars and a hamburger during the break for the two sets we played there. When it was my turn to order dinner, I asked the cute Dominican server to bring me a Swiss cheeseburger.

"Look, honey" she replied. "Your contract here is for five dollars and a hamburger. If we add cheese, you have to pay an extra dollar or we'll just take it out of your pay!"

That night I went home with four dollars, a cheeseburger in my belly, and a baffled idea of what my musical life would be in this city.

From then on, although I had never been a good business-man, I began to understand what Carmenchú Santana Vega meant when she said I had to find an economic equivalent to my work. And come to think of it, the restaurant we were leaving on the night she said that, was Home Restaurant on Manhattan's East Side.

Coda

Traveling, traveling, and always traveling like a bird, my dear Yeyito! In his work *The Insatiable Spider Man* Cuban author Pedro Juan Gutiérrez wrote, "I shut my eyes and again saw all those ducks, quacking, with their gorgeous, brilliant colors; shining in the golden light of the twilight, flying with joy and freedom!"

Olivier Messiaen composed beautiful music inspired by the million voices of birds, and Bird was the nickname of the great Charlie Parker. So that's why I have never favored keeping birds caged. No animal in general, actually, but especially the bird, which represents, precisely because of its makeup, the very symbol of freedom.

Some folks haven't raised their consciousness accordingly, such as my Cuban Jewish architect pal, who spoke to me like any exile (in his case a double whammy of an exile!), passionately and vehemently, about everyone's sacred right to freedom. He said this against the backdrop of an impressive wall at his New Jersey apartment, flanked completely, from side to side, with birdcages.

"Listen to Caruso chirp!" he gushed proudly, pointing to his favorite canary, singing of his pain from his gilded cage, like that sad fairytale.

Do unto others—and I include the Animal Kingdom here—as you would have others do unto you. My father taught me this when I was little. Although in life, and on occasion to be more pragmatic, you have to do certain things unto others before they do them to you, but then that's another story. In this context, it's important to note that whenever anyone commits a crime or action that goes against existing laws, the punishment is depriving that person of their freedom.

"If you don't behave, I sit you down and no playing in the street for you!" my old man threatened me frequently.

Also note that from infancy we learn, either the hard or easy way, that the loss or limitation of our right to move about freely is the most feared and effective punishment applicable. Therefore, this most basic right even for the poorest of men, and one for which the very rich pay dearly to exercise in typical high-end fashion, can only be lost through one's own fault.

Some people derive the greatest of pleasure from traveling great distances, be it on foot or through the most unorthodox methods of transportation, sometimes with hardly any money and taking on the harshest of jobs, just so they can reach destinations far and away from their native soil. This passion for travel becomes a real obsession with these fellows, among them, the humble author of these lines. Let me make clear that when I use the adjective "humble," I don't do it out of false or feigned modesty, but rather because once you begin to travel and encounter within yourself the enviable capacity for surprise, each day, by the grandeur and diversity of each country, any vestige of arrogance vanishes and loses its reason for being.

Fortunately, the nature of my work has offered me the opportunity to spend my time along roads, crossroads, and byways, in hostels (and hospitals) of every sort, ships, trains, carts pulled by horses and oxen, choppers, and planes. Airports? From Oklahoma to Haiti, to Singapore and Cuzco, passing through medieval Dubrovnik, Lebanon, Luanda, Oman, and Jerusalem. In the course of my travels I have met the most diverse and interesting people, whom I never would have dreamed of running into, and I have myriad friends spread throughout the world.

So, do I think it's worth it, to pursue a career as a musician? Did you ask me, Yeyo, if I am afraid of dying? Of course I am; I'm having too much fun down here, and although it is said that death is another kind of journey, I rather love this kind of journey down here, as a professional musician for more than sixty years. I've spent most of my life traveling to the most diverse regions of the world, meeting and working with amazing people, from great musicians, writers, dancers, and all kind of artists to exotic animal trainers and tourist guides on five continents. Traveling, for me, is more than just a way of earning my bread; it's also a passion, almost an obsession. So I've decided that while energy, health, and endurance are still with me, I'll keep traveling around and blowing these whistles I learned from my dad until my last breath.

"Remembering is to live again," sang Blanca Rosa Gil on that unforgettable bolero, so when my tired feet can no longer walk the pathways of Machu Picchu or the yellow paved streets of Sofia, or even lack the strength to board an airplane, I'll still have a clarinet and a phone to call the friends that are left. And when I run out of wind, I'll still keep a CD player and the memories of the beautiful places that have paraded in front of my eyes while looking through the window of a train or flying over the Andes. From that stage on the beach, with the ineffable George Benson, looking up at the mountains of Alicante, or over the monumental acoustic shell of Millennium Park in Chicago, or from the venerable stage of Carnegie Hall in New York, the city of my dreams.

But as I mentioned at the beginning of this long letter, retirement doesn't seem to be on my schedule any time soon, my dear old unknown friend Yeyito. So I hope someday our paths will cross, and finally, we'll find a couple of good reeds for the occasion and play a few notes together!

—*Paquito D'Rivera*

About the Author and Translator

Cuban-born clarinetist and saxophonist **Paquito D'Rivera** is celebrated for his artistry in Latin jazz and achievements in classical composition. He has received fourteen Grammys, the NEA Jazz Masters Award, and the National Medal of the Arts, among many others, and is the only artist to have won Grammys in both Classical and Latin Jazz categories. His oeuvre includes more than thirty solo albums. He lives in New Jersey.

* * *

Rosario Moreno is a Cuban-born bilingual translator, writer, creative director, and executive producer. A US Hispanic Market Specialist, she has worked for both the Univision and Telemundo networks and produced over one hundred TV commercials and programs, as well as numerous advertising and merchandising campaigns. She translates both from English to Spanish and from Spanish to English.

Restless Books is an independent publisher for readers and writers in search of new destinations, experiences, and perspectives. From Asia to the Americas, from Tehran to Tel Aviv, we deliver stories of discovery, adventure, dislocation, and transformation.

Our readers are passionate about other cultures and other languages. Restless is committed to bringing out the best of international literature—fiction, journalism, memoirs, poetry, travel writing, illustrated books, and more—that reflects the restlessness of our multiform lives.

VISIT US AT **WWW.RESTLESSBOOKS.COM**